THE VULNERABLE ALPHA

"Leading, motivating, and inspiring you to overcome adversity in your life and open the door to your true potential."

JEVON ALMOND

The Vulnerable Alpha

tellwell

Tellwell Talent
www.tellwell.ca

ISBN
978-0-2288-8882-6 (Hardcover)
978-0-2288-8883-3 (Paperback)
978-0-2288-8881-9 (eBook)

TABLE OF CONTENTS

PREFACE

Throughout my life, I've stayed consistently open to self-development. The desire for it comes easy, naturally, and flows like the energy all around us. If I can learn more about myself, the closer I'll be to finding fulfillment in life and understanding the journey. Negative and positive events have come into my life, and in my earlier years did not bring depression, which I have to be grateful for. My family dynamic has numbed me at times, and I'm feeling the full magnitude of its effect as I put my story on paper and share it with the world.

Energy is absolutely amazing to watch work its magic inside our own body, and to see its effect on people with whom we interact with each day. As a young child, I harnessed energy the best I knew how, and I've had to dig internally without grasping the understanding in order to survive. The truth is, I come from an incredibly dysfunctional and broken home, a very confusing and not-quite-suitable-for-the-dinner-guest-type conversation at the best of times. Are there far worse childhoods and upbringings? Absolutely. However, it's all about validating your own experience in life as it shapes the person you are and who you will become.

I've been a sponge all my life and I wouldn't have had it any other way. I aspire to lead, motivate, and inspire people whom I know very well, and I endeavour to enrich the lives of strangers I don't know at all. Thanks to a book called *The Big Leap* by Gay Hendricks, I realize that it's within my unique ability to tell the world my story. My goal is to make an everlasting positive change in anyone who feels challenged at some point in their own lives.

Lately I've moved into my zone of genius, to a state of never-felt-before euphoria and perspective, only to be knocked down into the reality check of processing my past. We all have a past; some run from it, and some repress it and block it completely, to the point of thinking that it will never need to be dealt with again. I used to think that was the case until I realized that my heart and mind were ready for the real thing, which would bring me to an emotional breaking point. I was living a lifestyle, my most ideal vision of how I wanted my life to be carried out, which would inevitably lead to happiness, abundance, success, and love. This is everything you need in life to thrive, in my opinion. Of course, food and shelter are a given, but these are the seeds to a life worth living, and I encourage you to focus all your energy on these things, and you will find greatness in yourself.

In my own life, these feelings prompted me to deal with my past. The broken home was no exaggeration. My mother, Anna, allowed my early childhood to feel like an emotional roller coaster, filled with motherly rejection and abandonment of me and my siblings. The sad truth is that her actions as a mother and human being have been recalibrated in my mind the only way I know how—as a lesson of what not to do. If I were to have children, her actions would unfortunately serve as a direct example on how you don't raise children.

Our mother would abandon me and my two sisters on what would become a sporadic disappearing act, typically taking place from Thursday night to about Tuesday morning. I've watched our own mother abandon and starve her children, and point a loaded rifle at my dad while telling him that he would die if he stepped foot in his own home to see his kids. I've witnessed my half-sister's father, Ross, and Anna beat each other bloody over drunken disputes while also exchanging malicious and disdainful comments with one another. At times late at night I'd hear high-pitched screams from Anna, and I honestly thought she'd been murdered by Ross, only to run out of my bedroom to see a blood stream running from our patio through the hallway carpet to the locked master bedroom door. Calling the police wasn't a luxury, as all phones seemed to be disconnected or coincidently disappeared at these common times of complete and utter chaos. As children we were forced to weep ourselves to sleep, not knowing if our mother had just been murdered. We had to starve and suffer the unpleasant curiosity of how to endure the next day.

Blocking these types of emotions is something that just happens over time. You become desensitized, lacking the basic understanding of how to feel things like love, emotional connection, vulnerability, and happiness. You're unable to enjoy the beautiful things life has to offer. Recently I've had to work through my past. This has inspired me to write *The Vulnerable Alpha*. I recommend it for everyone who feels some type of void in life or is curious about how to self-grow or heal internally. The Vulnerable Alpha is within all of us, it's the unbreakable beautiful part of our souls that have an endless amount of love for all of humanity. The Vulnerable Alpha is a mindset, it's resilience that is etched on your being and available for you to draw from at any point in your life you are dealing with substantial adversity. The Vulnerable Alpha within you is an internal compass of bringing your soul to the most harmonious state of equilibrium possible, while dealing with whatever is obstructing you in your path from achieving it. The Vulnerable Alpha is knowing there is a unique formula within your soul that makes you truly and uniquely incredibly special, and being your most authentic self is going to open that gateway to true vulnerability which inevitably reveals the most purposeful and fulfilling life you know was always what you wanted. The Vulnerable Alpha mindset is strength and determination to it's fullest expression, it's a mode that you are capable of that attracts all the abundance you've been searching for, and it was within you this entire time, always accessible.

It's very rewarding at this point in my life to work through my past trauma to become a better and more complete person. I'm not perfect, and nobody on this earth is. I've recently moved into a refreshed state of calmness, relinquishing the feelings of judgement, criticism, anger, frustration, maliciousness, and belligerence that ruled me. And although I had temporarily inherited high sensations of happiness, abundance, love, success, and positive energy, what I didn't know was that this would bring about a temporary subconscious confusion that led to numbness, emotional emptiness, anxiety, stress, and an overall loss of direction in life. Did I expect this to happen when I truly felt I had taken on the highest possible level of personal growth up to this point in my life? Absolutely not!

The fact is, you can't control what you haven't processed from your past. If you've been rejected, abandoned, or abused at any point in your life, you'll eventually have to process these compartmentalized feelings. Unfortunately, processing doesn't have a time limit or expiration date. When the human mind, heart and soul are ready to embrace one's past and deal with it head on, it will happen.

I've gone to the far depths of challenging my mind to understand who I really am. Up until my mid-thirties, I had never been depressed. I had always grasped large amounts of confidence, ambition, determination, resilience, and initiative in life. However, no matter how much of a lid you think you have on your own direction in life, you may have to take a back seat at some point to deal with your past. Everyone has a past, and the strongest minds decide to pursue their own history and heart to really understand what direction in life to take.

I believe that we all want to be mentally and emotionally unshackled so we can fully offer a bright, shining light to all those with whom we interact and love. I didn't have an easy childhood, but I had to learn at a young age how to mentally survive. I didn't make my physical and emotional needs a priority, as it was all about protecting my most valuable asset—the mind.

Starvation was common in my upbringing until the age of twelve, when I finally decided that enough was enough. I remember looking at Anna after she returned home from one of her standard drunken adventures while being an irresponsible mother. I was done, completely numb to any human emotion a child should be entitled to feel. The child parenting the mother—such a twisted perspective that you shouldn't have to endure at such a young age. Abandoned, rejected, love nowhere to be seen, I said that I was moving to Calgary to be with my dad. Her intoxicated and incoherent eyes suddenly became aware and competent for a mere few seconds, only to allow her to burst out in a drunken cry. It was sad, even as a child, to watch such an irresponsible human emotionally cave and show her son that she was really a young child inside who had never chosen the path of working through her past trauma and understanding negative behaviours, triggers, and patterns that kept her in the place she's likely still in today.

I share my own experiences as examples of how you can fight back in life, stick up for yourself, and go after what's rightfully yours in this world. We can maintain a resilient Vulnerable Alpha mindset while navigating a world of hurt and the negative circumstances that are forced upon us and out of our control. A very wise woman once told me that "you can't choose your family but you can choose your friends and community." These days that saying couldn't be more valuable and applicable as society continues to slip toward an unbalanced number of divorces and broken families. These days, a normal family is questionable to outsiders looking in. I wish it wasn't the case, but sadly, this is becoming the norm. Divorce rates are at their highest and on the rise, and many people get married for the wrong reason and bring children into this world that they're not prepared to support, nurture, and help raise into beautiful and emotionally healthy human beings. Instead, more often than not, children are raised with heart wounds that need to be processed in the future, because if left alone, they will only hinder the more complete and happier person from revealing themselves long-term.

I chose the title of this book because throughout my life I have fought back in efforts to not let my upbringing impede the life I want to live. I started reading self-development books when I was fourteen years old. I don't really know why or what for— I just felt compelled to do so. Looking for mentors to protect and grow my intellectually curious mind became the norm. It became a craving, a life worth chasing and living. I didn't yet know how to get what I wanted in life, but it became very apparent year over year that I wanted an ideal lifestyle, one that differed greatly from my upbringing, and one that would create a sense of validation as a human being. I realized that you can truly be the person you desire to be, and have anything you want in life. It doesn't matter if you came from a broken home or if you were physically or sexually abused as a child. "Whether you think you can, or think you can't—you're right," said Henry Ford.

In life, I chose to go after the bullies of life, to take on an Alpha, indestructible mindset of never letting anyone get the best of me. To never give up and keep going at all costs, to survive and endure life the best I can no matter what is thrown my way. To be able to get through the hardest of circumstances with raw spiritual strength, and to also know that being open and vulnerable as a human being is the path toward being full of love and abundance and living purposefully.

You'll always be turned down for certain jobs, denied a mortgage, told by your peers or even people who love you that you "can't" do something. Use this as your internal fuel for the fire, a motivation factor to prove them wrong. Be strong and stay open, find a way, and make it happen. Life will throw constant challenges your way, testing your ability to be Alpha as well as vulnerable. More people want to see you fail and deeply struggle before they ever want to see you succeed. It's etched in our makeup as human beings to have more negative energy, pessimism, and skepticism toward anyone who dances outside the norm of what is suitable for the common conformist. Be non-conventional. Chase life down the path less travelled, and I promise you that internal growth and strength waits for you at the finish line. Turn negative energy into positive, put the necessary habits in place to train your mind to think, feel, and breathe success and positive energy.

In the coming pages, I'd be privileged to take you on a journey of how I've been able to turn hardship, emotional emptiness, and abandonment into success, love, abundance, and the continuous pursuit of prolonged happiness and vulnerability. I'm pleased to give to you how I've been able to create my own internal support systems of positivity and strength so as to not let life's challenges hold me back. It's my mission within these pages to lead, motivate, and inspire you as a reader to overcome the adversity that is unique to you as a human being and to guide you toward your own special promised land. It's not an easy road, and it may get worse before it gets better, but you're never alone in this endeavour toward a valuable and fulfilling life, and your own mind, heart and soul are the most powerful instruments you possess.

CHAPTER 1

Childhoods Can Be Hard

"You are the sum total of everything you've ever seen, heard, eaten, smelled, been told, forgot- it's all there. Everything influences each of us, and because of that I try to make sure that my experiences are positive."
—Maya Angelou, *O, the Oprah Magazine*

I grew up in the small town/village of Kitscoty, Alberta, Canada and spent most of my childhood travelling between Lloydminster and Vermillion. We often drove to visit our grandparents in Derwent, or our uncle and aunt in Vegreville, which wasn't more than a couple of hours away.

I grew up with my full-sister, Addison, and my younger half-sister, Alice. At a very young age, we had to witness and endure the emotional consequences of our parents battling through an ugly divorce. They divorced because of infidelity, which unfortunately is becoming more and more common. Our mother, Anna, had met a man named Ross. They ended up together and had Alice.

Ross unfortunately died in a car crash before Alice was old enough to have a relationship with him. My father, Bob, was still trying to be a dependable dad and save the marriage; however, the spark was gone and it was just getting ugly.

Bob would stop by the house sometimes unexpectedly. Anna, still half drunk/high from the night before, would pull out one of Ross's rifles and point it straight at Bob, screaming that he'd be dead if he took one step inside the house. That was one of the handful of times I saw my dad cry. Unfortunately, you become desensitized to things like that during your childhood. They call it trauma or a heart wound, and we were unknowing recipients of these subconscious emotional wounds.

When my dad finally realized that the relationship was over, he moved to Calgary, Alberta and began working as a plumber to support himself very minimally. He sent the rest over to support us back home. I greatly admire how supportive of us our father was and still is. All his kids come first, now and forever, and I will always hold a deep respect for him in that regard. It's been embedded in my mind and will prepare me if I ever have the opportunity to have children in the future.

Unfortunately, Anna didn't show the same generosity, commitment, and loyalty toward her children during our upbringing. We lived on welfare at an early age, and it was difficult to understand why we didn't seem to live an ordinary life compared to most of our friends at school. Not having a lunch most days of the week, or a few dollars for pizza day at school every second Friday, was something you just got used to. My lunches usually consisted of a

Cheese Whiz and celery sandwich and a pack of raisins. At least it was something. At school I was called the "Fisher Price boy" or "Venture boy," as those were the less expensive brands and were deemed as "poverty labels." Sometimes this created anger and frustration for me as a child. I didn't understand why I had to be the outcast, or kid who was seen as living an abnormal lifestyle.

When Anna was going through the loss of Ross, and the loss of my dad, she really got into the liquor. She also often forgot that she had kids back at home, and would frequently abandon us without food for days at a time. Having no food, not knowing where your mother is, and living out of town on an acreage makes you grow up fast and not feel sorry for yourself. You have to become a survivor pretty quickly. You harden your character at a young age and adopt what I now know to be the "Stockdale principle." This principle states: "Know that you'll always prevail while still facing the brutal facts." Jim Collins, *Good To Great.*

At times I didn't know what was going to happen to us. I felt worthless as a child, but I knew deep down that we'd survive. The abandonment, starvation, and lack of parental guidance were the brutal facts. The light at the end of the tunnel was that I knew the day would come when I'd have a choice to never live the life I was currently enduring. I focused on the idea that I'd always prevail. It was a test of strength, and some premature character building that we didn't ask for but were forced to endure.

I vividly remember a day when Anna had taken me to her friend Lorne's place, which was approximately ten kilometres away from where we lived. I was starving when we arrived and there was nothing to eat. Anna gave me one of her empty promises, like "I'll only be a few minutes" or "I'm just going to say hi, and then we'll eat." What seemed like over an hour went by while I sat in the car and she drank in the garage with a bunch of strange men, and I began getting angry. I ended up getting out of the vehicle and telling her I wanted to go home. The strange men started laughing and told me to shut up and relax. Anna laughed along and played the game, as she subconsciously seemed to enjoy the attention from these people. She was seeking acceptance from men to a fault in that she prioritized these strangers over her own children.

I ended up playing with Lorne's dog for a while, trying to distract myself, and the dog ended up disappearing somewhere on the large property. I had no idea where it had gone, and all of a sudden, Lorne and Anna were scolding me and yelling and swearing, telling me to find the animal that was always unleashed.

I emotionally cratered. I burst into tears and walked back toward the car, but instead of going to the back seat, I turned toward the driveway and decided to walk barefoot back home. At seven years old, I walked approximately ten kilometres on a gravel road and crossed a major four-lane highway while starving, crying, and feeling abandoned and rejected by my own mother. I got near our home and had to raid our neighbour's garden for some carrots. Then I walked in the door to greet my older sister, Addison. I explained what happened, and I could see in her eyes that she couldn't let it faze her. She was teaching me how to be tough, harden up, and begin to internally protect myself so that I could come out of this in the future with at least some emotional strength. She was sharing the enduring experiences with me, and we were transforming into stronger survivors with each passing day.

From that point forward I mentally planned my exit strategy to get out of there at all costs and try to start a new life with my dad. Moving with my dad always felt like a way to rescue myself from the life I was currently living. It was intimidating to think of moving to a bigger city; however, I didn't care. I knew that as soon as the opportunity presented itself, I was out of there.

One morning Addison and I missed the bus to school, and Anna decided to teach us a lesson. We lived approximately ten kilometres west of Kitscoty and had a long two-hundred-metre driveway that the school bus would normally come down and turn around in. We would routinely watch for the bus intermittently while we gathered our things, and we'd time it perfectly to hop on when the driver turned around. Unfortunately, the new driver was early and didn't come down the driveway that day, so we ended up missing the bus. We had to wake Anna up from a drunk hangover to drive us to school, and she was livid.

We hopped into our white Chrysler Fifth Avenue and endured a tormenting drive to school. The ride was on gravel roads, and when you accelerate it's very easy to fishtail and potentially crash into the ditch. The ditches on the way into town were steeply V-shaped and filled with water overflowing from nearby dugouts and recent rainfall, so a crash and potential rollover could mean big trouble for the three of us. Anna was completely vexed, yelling and swearing while incoherently accelerating, fishtailing, and jerking the steering wheel. It was one of the scariest days of my childhood. I thought we were going to die and was absolutely terrified. It taught me the valuable lesson to never miss the bus, especially if you have to rely on an alcoholic to drive you to school.

It doesn't take too many undesirable events like that until you know it's time to get out of the situation you're in at all costs. I was very fortunate in that I had the opportunity to leave and go to what I thought would provide a more stable life with my dad, and I planned on timing it appropriately. When Anna came back from one of her typical drunken adventures that lasted anywhere from two to four days, I was ready to tell her the news. We lived in a bi-level where you'd walk into the front entry landing and up a set of stairs to the main floor or down a set of stairs to the basement. I was waiting in the front entry landing when she walked in. Even still buzzed, she could see it in my eyes.

"I'm moving in with dad, Anna." She could tell it was a conviction for me, and she burst into tears. I kind of half hugged her while she cried, and I stayed strong by telling myself, *You will prevail, Jevon; you'll survive and one day build a great life for yourself somehow, someway.*

I was in Grade 5 that year, and when the school year was over, Anna drove me to the Greyhound station, hugged me, and walked away crying. I watched her as she turned and walked out of the station. The same abandonment sensation she'd made me feel many times before no longer put tears on my face. I was escaping the nightmare. I think back now and wonder what thoughts were going through her head at that moment.

I always gravitated toward my dad when I was young. His sense of stability, calm demeanour, and simplified mannerisms gave me a sense of security in what was a very chaotic upbringing. He's a very happy-go-lucky, selfless man who puts everyone he cares about before himself at all costs. He once told me that he'd rather have ten dollars in the bank and one hundred friends versus ten friends and one million dollars in the bank. Although I don't agree with the exact calculation, I could understand what he was saying. He cared less about monetary gain or status and most about the people around him.

Whenever he could, our dad would visit us during Christmas holidays or for some of my hockey tournaments. I remember staring out our living room window for hours on end waiting until I could see his red van pass a certain point about one kilometre out from our home. I'd be ecstatic once I saw it. When he'd leave, I'd stare out the window, watching his red van pass the same point, and afterward I'd cry for hours in a fetal position. It felt like a stab to the heart every time he left without taking me with him out of what felt like a living hell. I was dead inside, and his visits were the only ray of light in my childhood life. One time I snuck into his van after he said his goodbyes to everyone. I lay hid in the back all the way until we were probably near Edmonton, and then I peeped up, knowing that I was probably going to get in serious trouble. I don't remember him getting angry at me at all; he just turned around and drove me back home, having a better idea of the deep inner struggle I was dealing with.

I was also very fortunate to be put into hockey when I was younger, and I knew how lucky I was that part of his financial support for me and my sisters went toward a sport that I could enjoy. I'm very grateful for it, as it was a way to escape and distract myself from the life I lived. I experienced a sense of teamwork, camaraderie, and excitement.

When I was around nine years old and there were giant snowbanks in our driveway from a blizzard the night before, I'd bundle up and get up at 5:00 a.m. and shovel the gravel driveway for over an hour so that we could get me to my 7:00 a.m. hockey practice. I needed the escape in so many ways. It was one of the only sanctuaries of my youth, and I tapped into it as much as possible. I wasn't a very technically skilled hockey player when I was younger, but I had so much energy and enthusiasm that it kept me moving on the ice. I hadn't scored a goal all year, and when my dad showed up for a tournament, I yearned to make him as proud as I could. I crashed myself and the puck into the net during two breakaways, and they both counted as goals. It wasn't pretty, but it meant the world for me to make him proud. My teammates couldn't believe it. "Showing off for pops," they'd say.

I moved to Calgary before Grade 6 started, and a new chapter of my upbringing began. I was now living with my dad; however, I also met the Wild family for the first time. My dad had been dating a woman named Dalinda for quite some time, and she had four kids: Curtis, Jared, Larissa, and Dwayne. When I arrived, I ended up moving in with them into a small five-bedroom bi-level in the community of Glamorgan. My oldest half-brother, Charles, whom my dad had from his previous marriage with Tammara, was also living in the same home, and I ended up sharing a room with him. Larissa was upstairs in one bedroom, Dalinda and my dad in the other bedroom upstairs, and the gang of boys downstairs.

I soon realized it was another chapter of big city survival, as my dad was very much preoccupied with trying to run the now mixed family, and enduring all the stresses that came along. I tried my best to get along with everyone and ended up bonding the most with Jared and Dwayne. Larissa, Curtis, and Charles were older than me by over five years, and Dwayne, Jared, and I were within three years of each other. And so the mischievous tripod was born. We had a lot of fun and created a lot of troublesome adventures together.

It was very much a fend-for-yourself early teenage upbringing. Money was scarce back then, although we had capitalistic opportunities on our side. We'd take the bottles in whenever possible, or we'd go to Safeway and help people with their groceries, hoping to take the cart back and receive a quarter. After a few hours, it would usually generate enough money to buy lunch at Taco Bell, which was an enjoyable reward.

We'd often go to what we called the "sand dunes," which was a private property area for a landscape company to store and transport various types of dirt in the Signal Hill area of the city. We'd hang out there for hours on end, like it was a do-or-die mission, trying to build lookouts and small partial caves in an attempt to not be seen by the dump trucks that came in and out.

I was a troublemaker in my early days in Calgary. I lacked discipline and exploited the many opportunities a mischievous child has while simultaneously trying not to get caught. I also faced enormous peer pressure from my friends to perform vandalism, light things on fire, do drugs, and steal—all for the thrill of the moment and the excitement that comes along with it. I resorted to stealing from businesses and vandalizing property, all for the thrill and excitement of the experience. Looking back, those aren't my proudest moments, but I was an unguided and incredibly rebellious young teenager. I didn't have a teacher or role model to fall back on, and it was evident that I was heading toward even worse trouble if I didn't change my ways. It was only inevitable that I'd end up with a juvenile record, or dead.

Another individual who created toxicity in my teenage years before taking her own life was my would-be stepmother, Dalinda Wild. She was to the core a very vicious and manipulative woman who was out to destroy the spirit of anyone in her path at all costs. Unfortunately, upon my arrival in Calgary to escape my own version of hell, she viewed me as an obstacle in the way of the family dynamic she was living with her kids and my father. At first she was artificially warm toward me and the idea that I was moving in to become part of the family, and everything would be at perfect equilibrium. This was one of the biggest misconceptions and misjudgements of character I've ever experienced when meeting someone. Dalinda viewed me as a threat from day one, concerned that my dad would now be giving me energy and attention, resulting in a loss of energy and attention toward her and her four kids. She despised me and tried to manipulate my dad into believing that this wasn't the case, yet our direct conversations with each other would show me how malicious and belligerent she could really be.

It was subconsciously devastating for me to have one terrible chapter of female parenthood—which included starvation, abandonment, and rejection—followed by another that was a different combination of disdain, resentment, manipulation, and hatred. Unfortunately, it was evident that parental figures, especially female role models, in my life were not blessed with positive or nurturing qualities, and I was going to have to deal with radically accepting this hurtful truth and doing my best to survive and then learn to thrive in my later years.

CHAPTER 2

You Can Always Turn It Around

"All good is hard. All evil is easy. Dying, losing, cheating and mediocrity are easy. Stay away from easy."
—Scott Alexander

My teenage years were filled with rebellion, anger, and the constant challenge of learning how to channel my ambition and leadership traits. It didn't end up working out with the mixed family under the same roof, so my dad, Charles, and I ended up moving into a two-bedroom condo in the community of Glamorgan. This area was known as my stomping grounds from Grade 6 all the way up to the beginning of high school.

In Grade 6, I was incredibly rebellious to anyone and everyone. Charles was dealing with the responsibility of having a newborn baby with Dalinda's daughter, Larissa. When their son Jerome was born, Charles was fifteen and Larissa fourteen, which put a strain on my dad and Dalinda in terms of upcoming financial support.

In elementary school, I was the bad, delinquent kid, prematurely diagnosed with ADD by teachers at school. I had an infinite amount of energy and was very intense. I'd do silly things in class, like put a lighter to one of our teacher's flammable hair spray bottles in the back of the classroom to create a mini flame burst, all for a little thrill and excitement. Even though our teacher was absent from the classroom, it was inevitable that she'd find out, and I was suspended for a day. I didn't stop there. I got into fights with two sets of brothers that seemed to pick on and bully other kids throughout our school. I'd just go after them when I saw that, and already having a not-so-stellar reputation in the discipline department, I was suspended again for three days. I'd bully the bullies, or at least I'd try, at the risk of my own rebellious demise. My behaviour would lead to another three-day suspension, and then a five-day suspension. I hadn't even made it to junior high school yet, and I was close to getting expelled from elementary school.

My teacher Mrs. Mclaren, who was a wonderful, very strong woman, pulled me aside and said, "This is the real deal, Jevon. What are you going to do when you get expelled?"

I'd get sent home early, suspended from school, and be excited to have the day off, so I'd perform more mischief. My dad would come home and look at me, knowing that I'd been suspended again without any exchange of words needing to take place. He would say later say to me, "If you get expelled from school, you have to get a real job like the rest of us." I'd always reassure him that it wasn't going to happen, although even I knew I was right on the brink of losing a free public education because of my actions.

I remember playing soccer during lunch hour and getting in an altercation with another student, named Tim. I realized that expulsion was the definite repercussion if I fought back, so I let Tim take free shots at me and pretty much kick my ass so I could avoid being expelled. I couldn't lay a hand on him, and it took tremendous discipline that I didn't know I possessed not to fight back. Fortunately for me, word got back to our principal that I didn't fight back, and my punishment was reduced back to another five-day suspension.

It was around that time in my life that I realized that the path I was on wasn't a good one at all. No one was going to make the necessary changes to my own life but me. I had to change my behaviour in order to change the direction in my life, so I started to make slow, subtle changes toward becoming a more disciplined and responsible human being. It wasn't an easy process, and a lot of the time I'd take one step forwards and then two steps back. I tried taking the initiative to do what the good kids did. I tried becoming a crosswalk patroller to help kids cross the street at lunch time or after school. I figured this was a step in the right direction, but the lead patroller knew I was bad news and initially turned me down. I applied my persistence in a positive way and realized that I wouldn't be denied. I showered her with kindness and eventually got on as a patroller, holding the stop sign and allowing younger kids to cross the street safely. I ended up trying harder in school and was rewarded for it. I received a gold pencil, which was awarded to a student each month of the year, and this was a big deal to keeners. I was now keen to stand out in the areas I could and try to change the rebellious and mischievous habits I'd developed throughout my upbringing.

In junior high, I changed the group of friends I hung out with and tried to get in with a more disciplined group of people, whom at the time I named "the nerds." I wanted to be a nerd badly if it meant being awarded for positive behaviour. I realized that I had the opportunity to no longer seek negative recognition from my peers, but now I could seek positive recognition. It became an addiction to try my best not only for myself but the people around me. I slowly went from grades well below 50 per cent to aspiring to make the honour roll in Grade 9. It was a big challenge, as I had a steep hill to climb and my teachers had already pegged me with the well-deserved label of a troubled youth with little hope.

Learning my ability to be a salesman even at a very young age, I was adamant to sway them. I treated each subject like I now do in business, with the pursuit of being the best I can be. I'd ask each of my teachers what I could do better and what specific areas I needed to improve on. Even stopping in for help after school became a regular occurrence for me in order to substantially bump up my grades and start to prepare for this daunting "future," as adults would verbalize.

Teachers and my peers began to notice my change in demeanour. All of a sudden, I had an optimistically positive scholastic agenda. Teachers began to warm to the idea that this kid wanted to figure out how to be better. I eventually ended up making the "Roll of Merit," as every one of my grades was above 80 per cent for that specific reporting period. Although I aimed high, to go from below the fifties to over ninety, I had to be happy with almost getting there. In Grade 9 I ended up winning the Alfred Ernest Cross award at my junior high school, A.E. Cross, for being the most improved student of the year. I went up on stage to receive my award, and at that moment I knew I was on a serious track toward the pursuit of breaking the pattern in which I grew up. I thought about everything I did to create the opportunity to receive that award, and how empowering and confident it made me feel at that moment. It was the biggest victory of my life up to that point, and it felt great.

When I reflect on my scholastic experiences as a young kid and teenager, I think of what valuable lessons I learned over the years. I think back to whose advice and teaching techniques really made a lasting, positive impression on me outside of the classroom. My chemistry teacher, Mr. Kendall, who taught at the time over at Central Memorial High School, was a strong-willed, hard-nosed teacher. His philosophy was, "If you're going to fail my class, then get out right now." I liked that black and white approach to how he taught; it demanded respect and was bad ass. He was a no nonsense teacher and wanted everyone in his classroom to over-achieve expectations set on themselves for chemistry. He somehow was able to facilitate a different set of circumstances for each student to motivate them individually to succeed.

As high school was still a struggle for my entrepreneurial and energetic mind, I found it very hard to focus and pay attention to my peers. I made the mistake on a few occasions of not completing my homework assignments or practice quizzes the night before because I was learning what commitment really meant. Chasing girls and playing video games took up most of my evening time, and it was hard to fit in time for chemistry homework. I sat at the front right-hand side of the classroom near the entrance door. I'd been moved there on a past occasion because I was distracting myself and other students as a "mid row" student. I wasn't successful there, and Mr. Kendall knew it, so he made an immediate adjustment and "promoted" me, as I like to say, to the front of the classroom.

After asking everyone for their homework, he asked me where mine was. I told him I wasn't able to complete it. I had just received one of the lowest scores in the class on a prior exam, and Mr. Kendall was livid. He pulled me aside into the chemistry supply room and made sure the door was open for the rest of the students to hear. I remember that moment vividly. He said, "Jevon, you got one of the lowest scores in the class on our past quiz, and you didn't do your homework!?" The entire class could hear, and I immediately felt embarrassed for my actions. He went on to say, "If you aren't committed, I don't want you in my classroom, and we may as well send you to the office to be withdrawn."

I explained to him that I wanted to stay in the class and would put in more effort to do my best to exceed his expectations. I never ended up acing that course, but I can tell you I passed, and he got the most out of me at that time in my life as a student. After much reflection, I realized I wasn't so much embarrassed as I was disappointed in myself for a lack of commitment and effort. He helped reveal to me that I wanted to win and be a successful person in life. He wouldn't tolerate anything else. A very powerful lesson, and a truly exceptional teacher he was. I called him years later to thank him for everything.

CHAPTER 3

Suicide

"If you're going through hell, keep going."
—Winston Churchill

It's heartbreaking when people take their own lives. We all know of someone, whether it be a friend or family member or person in the community, who has taken their own life. Dwayne Wild, whom I considered my stepbrother, even though Bob and Dalinda never married, took his own life on June 17, 2008. I wasn't extremely close with Dwayne during the period in which he took his life, but it was a hard loss for many people who knew him, including myself. His mother, Dalinda, couldn't bear the pain and ended up taking her own life less than a few years later. These were family tragedies, and they took their toll on all the lives these two people touched. Although I hadn't experienced depression up to that point in my life, I imagined that it would feel like the opposite end of the spectrum of being motivated, inspired, and confident with things in life. If all those feelings were on the other end of the spectrum, I can understand why suicide would be a consideration for many people struggling with hard times and adversity.

I used to drive Dwayne to school every day in high school, and drive him home afterward as well. I sometimes go back to those days and remember how reserved he was and how he always had a wealth of obscure facts, especially to do with insects and reptiles. I remember the day of his funeral, when everyone grieved at his grave site and I was emotionless, just trying to make sense of my life up to that point. I already had so much trauma compartmentalized inside from my earlier years, and I'd convinced myself that revealing it would be weak. I wasn't in touch with my vulnerability at that time, and for obvious reasons. I waited for everyone to leave except for a close friend, Brian. Then I kneeled at the grave and let out all my emotion for Dwayne so that he knew how much he meant to me.

I've tried my best to be optimistic and believe that the people who decide to take this path are now in a better place. I often think about what I could have done differently, or if this still would have happened had I been a more available and involved mentor in his life during the key moments of his deepest struggles and challenges. A friend I'd known since elementary school, David Stone, also took his own life in 2011, and that was very unfortunate as well. We played hockey and grew up together, and it just plays in my mind that had our friendship been stronger throughout the years, perhaps I could have picked up on his difficulties in life. It's why I write these words, to show people who deal with adversity in life, whether it be any type of abuse, depression, or neglect, that you can rise up from it and make your own personal transformational comeback. No matter where you are, you *can* do it. You could be broke, alone, cold, helpless, and homeless on the street right now, or addicted to drugs or in a dire-straits abusive relationship or upbringing, and feel there is no way to get out. You can ask for help and find ways to confront these challenges and learn and grow from them in order to put them behind you. It definitely will be a challenge; however, with applied therapy and awareness tools, you can reach a better place mentally. It's also important to find the cheerleaders of your life, because there is someone out there who will have your back, no matter how bad it gets. Someone will be there, and if nobody is there, I'm there for you and I see you and know it's undeniably hard.

When I watched the show *Intervention* a handful of times, I didn't really know what to think in terms of the validity of the events and how much they were altered to allow for more of a "dramatic" affect. It never really struck a chord until I had to do it in my own life with our mother, Anna. Anna unfortunately seemed to have decided to never grow up due to her own patterns, triggers, and behaviours from her childhood. She constantly experimented with all types of drugs while raising Addison, Alice, and I, and she never seemed to desire taking responsibility for her own children or her actions. She was in a complete freefall as a human being in terms of her addictions, and she had likely relinquished the idea of being a grown adult and making something for herself well before I was born.

We were on welfare at a very young age, and around the time Ross died, the wheels fell off completely and for good in terms of my mother's emotional ability and desire to be a nurturing person. Looking back, I try to show compassion for how hard it must have been to lose Ross, as despite their relationship being so toxic, I knew they loved each other immensely. This definitely took its toll on me and my sisters. I remember one night vividly, when Anna and Ross were screaming and swearing foul maliciousness and belligerence at each other while intoxicated, and as a child feeling nothing but deep internal pain and sorrow. The hurt that night of radically accepting how dysfunctional and flawed my current circumstances were pushed me to attempt to run away. Not even in Grade 3, I committed to actually trying to get myself out of that awful hell. We lived on an out-of-town acreage, and it was dark and into the early hours of the morning by this time, but I still had to try. Where I was going and to whom I would reach out for help was unknown for me, as my only thought was to get out.

I packed up some basics in terms of clothing, and I didn't really know how to prepare for this. It was a lot to ask of a young child, but I was trying to survive elsewhere and determine what bare essentials I'd need. I grabbed my toothbrush, toothpaste, and some hockey cards, as I thought I could sell them for money. It was my only strategy for finances at the age of seven, and I was now ready to leave.

I went to Addison's room and asked her if she was coming. She looked at me calmly and told me to go to bed. I could tell she thought the idea was ridiculously futile, but it didn't matter to me. For some reason my sister seemed to be more willing, or perhaps more numb, to endure the very unfortunate circumstance we were in, and she didn't quite demonstrate the desire for a different environment the same way I did. I couldn't bear it, and I longed for a better life that we weren't capable of getting if we didn't influence or change our circumstances. I didn't know what "more fulfillment" looked like, but I had to try to find it somehow.

Still determined, I went outside into the pitch-black night to the sound of coyotes howling in the distance. Out on an acreage with no lights around except for only a few neighbouring home's porch lights, I was terrified and could feel my bones trembling with fear. I packed everything into my trusty red wagon and began to make the trek down our long gravel driveway as I cried and looked at the sky, wondering when help would arrive. There unfortunately was no special delivery. I remember the sound of the gravel squishing against the soles of my shoes as I took each step toward the end of the driveway; it was louder than my weeping. I was completely numb and had emotionally collapsed. I was beyond broken, and my soul was on life support, propped up by my inner spirit. I felt like a dead soul in a young boy's body.

I reached the end of the driveway and was so frightened that I jumped into the ditch, shivering and feeling sorry for myself. Self pity as a child or adult is still a bitch. Help didn't arrive that day, as my sister told Anna that I was running away, and she came outside and collected me at the end of the driveway in the ditch. I don't think I would have been able to get much farther that night, but the seed was planted to create a better life for myself at all costs. The exit strategy from this terrible circumstance had begun manifesting itself in my mind. It's an unfortunate thing to experience, and I know I'm not alone in this feeling. Not being nurtured, but instead being starved and abandoned for days at a time, created long-term, embedded trauma that I'd find out later in life had to be processed via professional therapy.

Well into my teenage years, Anna's psychologically disturbing alcohol induced tendencies resurfaced in the worst ways. She would try to create drama in all areas of our lives, and she seemed to require a daily quota to be satisfied. After many disturbing episodes in which she acted out her mental imbalances by perpetually disrupting our lives, we decided to have an intervention. It's extremely hard to sit down and explain from the bottom of your heart that your mother needs professional help in the worst ways. Anna also threatened to take her own life many times, and this was a huge concern for us. She suffered from heart issues and was on different medications, which she liked to mix with alcohol. This was a recipe for disaster and something we were severely concerned would push her over the edge. Unfortunately, you can't admit someone into the hospital if they're unwilling and not noticeably suicidal. This basically meant that if she wasn't suicidal in front of police or hospital representatives, then we couldn't admit her without consent. We continuously tried to get her help, and eventually she agreed to admit herself into the psych ward for assessment. In life you will experience instability and meet suicidal people. Some will take their own lives, and some won't. At the end of the day, if you feel you tried your best to help these people, then you can't carry guilt. This is one of the unfortunate parts of life that we have to overcome and find peace with.

I have friends who grew up dealing with sexual abuse as young kids and ended up as successful human beings as well as business owners and philanthropists. We all have the opportunity to do amazing things in this life, and we also get down at times. If at any time you or anyone you know is dealing with adversity or struggles in life that are too difficult to bear, please reach out and ask for help. It's the biggest gift you could give yourself or someone you care for. Whether it be suicide, sexual, mental, or physical abuse, or even depression, starvation, or abandonment, you are not alone in your battle to overcome these obstacles. We can overcome these barriers together.

CHAPTER 4

Fall in Love with Rejection

"Effort only fully releases its reward
after a person refuses to quit."
—Napoleon Hill

Have you ever had someone tell you that you can't do something? Of course you have; we've all experienced this when it comes to achieving our goals and pursuing our unique paths in life. Pursuing your dreams at all costs, regardless of what other people think about you or your endeavour, is the ultimate mindset goal. It's about achieving the end result and striving toward that ultimate fruition of your own special dream. Throughout my life, I've dealt with many obstacles that impeded my success as an athlete, entrepreneur, and human being. There will always be obstacles in our lives to overcome.

One of my earlier memories of falling in love with rejection occurred when I was younger. I grew up near a tiny little town called Kitscoty, maybe the population of a few hundred people. It's near the border city of Lloydminster, which sits right in the middle of the Alberta/Saskatchewan border. It was the small town where drivers intersecting with each other would wave and show their gratitude toward one of their own community citizens. You rarely see this in the beautiful city I now call home—Calgary, Alberta. In elementary school, the niche was so small that the "well put together" families were well known, and so were the "dysfunctional" families, throughout the town and surrounding areas.

My sister and I were known as the "welfare" kids, and even hearing that word still lights a fire inside me with tenacity as I write these words. On the bus to school, I'd get the daily heckling from one of my fellow schoolmates about my Fisher Price lunch kit and backpack. Yes, I was known as the "Fisher Price boy." It was devastating at the time, but little did I realize a fire was burning inside of me, saying, "Fall in love with rejection, Jevon. You'll be so much stronger and resilient for it in the future." So I did, and I continued with that perspective throughout my childhood years. I played on the local baseball team and remember being called the "Venture" glove kid, which meant my glove wasn't the highest end. I knew we were poor, and it sucked at the time, but I'm grateful for experiencing a lack of abundance in my life during those lean years. It only made attracting abundance, success, love, and happiness into my life that much more gratifying when I focused on attaining those desires. We all are going to deal with some form of rejection at various points of our lives. It's how we react to these situations that is the most rewarding to our personal growth and self-development.

From a career and entrepreneurial perspective, that's when I really learned to fall in love with rejection even more. My upbringing taught me to develop wisdom very quickly—that's what growing up fast does to you! It gives you thicker skin and teaches you how to tap into your internal resilience so that when circumstances don't go your way, they don't drag you down. As a young teenager, I started to goal set, repeatedly writing down what I wanted in life at that particular time: retire by thirty, own multiple properties, and own multiple businesses. I knew the vehicle I'd be driving and the geographical locations throughout the world where I'd own properties. I started painting this picture early. This manifestation spawned a curiosity and strategic mindset at a young age that would lead me to doing and inquiring about many things that most young people just don't do or have an interest in.

I started asking my dad at the age of seventeen how I could buy a property. I asked him if he thought I could qualify for a mortgage somehow. He said something I'll never forget that day: "Jevon, you have the mind of a forty year old living in a seventeen year old's body." I thought that was pretty bad ass, to be honest, and it inspired me even more. I kept asking questions, and my very honest father said, "I'm not going to be able to give you the answers you seek, Jevon. You're going to have to go out and get them yourself."

I was frustrated with his bluntness at the time, feeling rejected by my own father when asking for wisdom. It didn't take long, however, for me to appreciate the gift he'd given me. I can go out and find the answers on my own. What a beautiful thing! So I did. I started calling realtors and asking about properties that I had no business being able to buy as a teenager, as I was still finishing high school and preparing for college. I was aspiring toward a business, marketing, and management degree. That ended up being short-lived, which I'll get to. I'd visit financial planning offices, such as Edward Jones, and listen to the financial planner tell me to diversify and plan long-term to become very wealthy. At the time I found the conversation somewhat humorous, because Robert Kiyosaki, one of my valued mentors, had just had taught me in the book *Rich Dad Poor Dad* that financial planners will tell you to diversify and invest for the long-term, but often they don't follow their own investment advice! My desperately ambitious teenage mind had a good chuckle after I left the office. I started calling mortgage brokers, asking about what I needed to do to qualify for properties. I began to read real estate books, such as *Real Estate Riches*, and go to real estate seminars, trying to understand how to create "positive cash flow," as Mr. Kiyosaki so eloquently verbalized.

It didn't take long for me to start getting kicked in the face with rejection from family, peers, and even various professionals when seeking their expertise. "You're way too young son," "Call me when you have a job," "Don't waste my time," "You aren't ready to be a property owner," "Own a business? You're not done school yet; focus on that first." In some ways they were right, or so I thought. *Am I really crazy to be trying to learn this all at such a young age? Or am I really onto something here with fast tracking my success path in an expedited and aggressively ambitious manner?* I chose the latter. I was the guy who would ask you a question ten different ways, trying to get an answer other than no. I was a sales person and loved negotiating with people to find an eventual yes. I was undeniably persistent with burning desire and focus within me, and I showed it in all my encounters.

Fast-forward a few years to the age of twenty-one. I had a portfolio of about five properties: a few renovation flip deals, a revenue-generating property, a condo being built in the downtown Calgary core, and a larger triple-car-garage estate home being built in the town of Chestermere by a custom builder. I was beyond relentless to be successful, and although I didn't have the wisdom I do today, my tenacity was intense, and my hunger to succeed and never have to re-live my upbringing of poverty was too vividly powerful for me to stop. The most important thing to note about rejection is that it can be interpreted with either optimism or skepticism. It's really up to you. I always choose optimism and positivity over any self-doubt or pessimism that I won't be able to succeed. It's something you can tap into with your own mind and kick out the negative energy as soon as it starts to radiate in. Not all endeavours will work out the way you want them to as you're attaining wisdom, so learn to harness your ambition through the younger years of development. That's what becoming successful is all about—making mistakes along the way and not letting them hinder your positive perspective. Eventually you learn to mute the rejection and push harder toward your goals, dreams, desires, and vision of how you want your lifestyle to unfold.

CHAPTER 5

Survival Mode

"A time comes when you need to stop waiting for the man you want to become, and start being the man you want to be."
—Bruce Springsteen

At a young age, dealing with substantial adversity, you can either let it consume your world and bring on self pity and a feeling of victimization, or you can learn to tap into your inner resilience. Unfortunately, at a young age it's hard to understand that surviving is resilience, strength and courage, showing faith when things look bleak and hopeless. Being perpetually starved, abandoned, and rejected by our mother, I had to turn on a switch called "survival mode." Anyone currently reading this who has dealt with any type of abuse for a prolonged period of time knows exactly how it feels. You lock away your emotions, with a combination code around your heart, and form a concrete barrier that can withstand any type of physical or verbally abusive attack. The last thing we're worried about at the time is where the key or code will be for us to open it later in our lives, when we actually do find beauty and abundance in ourselves and other people. It doesn't matter at that current time; it's all about surviving.

I know the feeling well, and you're never alone in this fight to survive. The thing about survival mode is that it's such a beautiful and inspiring thing to endure. It's one of your greatest secret weapons as you battle through any type of adversity in life. It gives you the tools to succeed in so many ways as you grow up and acquire more wisdom and maturity. Eventually, you realize that it was resilience after all, and it's now a virtue that belongs to you for the rest of your life, allowing you to take your appetite for a more success-infused life to another level. Embrace the adversity, let it put a smile on your face, and know that it's making you stronger, setting you up for a more progressive curve of finding the lifestyle you dream of, surrounded by people who love you, and whom you love.

Throughout my life I've been able to strive toward my goals, focus on the law of positivity, and attract abundance into my life. I've been very fortunate to start a business at a young age and have it continue to grow as I try to share the lessons learned throughout the duration of my life thus far. I attribute the hunger and determination I have to achieve my ideal lifestyle to the way I was raised. It provided me an internal fire that I don't think could have as easily been replicated had I come from an upbringing filled with far less adversity. That's why I'd never want to be handed a real estate empire, or a multi million-dollar business, by any family member, as one would already have to possess expedited virtues capable of sustaining the current business models and taking them to the next level. Many successful people have inherited their parent's businesses and increased the prosperity within that business even more, and I love hearing about those success stories. But the opposite also occurs, where someone inherited a business that they weren't mentally prepared for and lacked the humility, diligence, ambition, mental fortitude, and resilience to propel forward, and it floundered. I believe that regardless of our upbringing, adversity or not, we decide how we develop our traits and personality characteristics to evolve and adapt to unpredictable and abrupt changes. My life circumstances forced independence, in that I was going to have to be in charge of creating my own mental mindset that would set me up for future success in all areas of life. You have to prepare for unpredictability in your life and build yourself up so strong that you have no choice but to pounce on the opportunities life will throw your way.

Back to throwing away the survival mode key locked around your heart. Have you wondered why you've been able to survive and even thrive all these years, achieve many lifestyle- and health-oriented goals, yet your most intimate relationships have been in a prolonged state of suffering or not as harmonious as you'd like? Through some very beautiful relationships with amazing human beings, I learned that I wasn't able to find the key to my emotional vulnerability and unlock the vault. This has caused unnecessary heartache for some of the most important people I love. Although my heart was in the right place, the walls are very hard to break down for me to truly show my vulnerability and full emotional expression to those dearest to my heart.

In order to give your heart and full expression to the incredibly special ones you love along the way, you have to trigger an emotional breakthrough and shatter those barriers around your self-protection mechanisms that helped you throughout your journey, but are no longer needed. Eventually you're going to be all strong and mighty, where you don't need to worry about surviving, because you're now living the lifestyle you truly desire and have the woman or man of your dreams in front of you. But you won't be able to give yourself to them because of these walls. I want to do everything in my power to allow you to have this breakthrough together with your partner and truly be vulnerable to them and show them your true expression and how much you love them. Meditate together, volunteer together, read books to each other, have candlelight yoga together to tap into that breakthrough and showcase your undeniable love for your soul mate. This can be done without running away from your partner just because you fear that they'll leave you first.

Survival mode is a beast inside of you that protects you, but eventually you're going to have to kill the beast who protects your heart and give it to the rightful owner—yourself and your soul mate/life partner. Trust me, this will be one of the hardest things in your life, bringing you back to the vulnerability you had before you locked away your full emotional expression and threw away that precious key. Conventional traditional therapy or spiritual enlightenment may trigger the breakthrough, but I don't recommend relying on this alone. Focus on your self-development and build up your personal growth by learning more about how you tick, what makes you happy, what lifestyle you truly desire, and the partner you're most compatible with. Spending time alone will also give you answers about yourself that no form of therapy will tap into. There's something significant about your own solitude in terms of self-transformation and personal evolution.

Once you have that person in your life, don't let them go, and make sure that you break through your shell and love them to the fullest, because after surviving the adversity, what a let down it would be not to share with your soul mate, the one who saw the diamond in the rough and fell in love with you and allowed your walls to light on fire and fall to the ground. Get emotional and cry with your partner. I don't care how tough or strong you think you are—the last thing you want to do is be too emotionally stoic, when all they want to see is that you aren't actually a robot and locked up emotionally. Men usually aren't very honest or exploratively open about their emotional position with most things, especially relationships. We think staying alpha means refusing to be vulnerable. It's actually the complete opposite—the more vulnerable you are as a human, the more Alpha your spirit and soul are in terms of empowerment and authentic zest for life and love. During your own transition you may feel weak, vulnerable, or like the walls are falling and it will be one of the most terrifying and chaotic moments you've had to endure yet in your life, but I promise that it will also be one of the most rewarding. This is the way to experiencing true love and full expression with yourself and who you choose as a partner. I've been guilty of staying emotionally locked up and unavailable in some of the most special and loving relationships, and I want to help get you to the promised land by learning from my own process, which I'm grateful to share.

CHAPTER 6

Utilize Your Support System

"A small team of A-Plus players can run circles around a giant team of B and C players."
—Steve Jobs

In a perfect world, we'd all be close with each one of our family members, with an unbelievably beautiful and unbreakable bond of love. Sadly, this isn't the case, as many families are very close to normal, and many are few and far between. The sooner you realize and accept that your support system may not always be just your family, the more successful your self-development will be in the long-term. It's not always super exhilarating knowing that I don't have a close relationship with my mother or father; however, it has allowed me to cultivate other very powerful, nurturing relationships with those around me. This is an absolute necessity if adversity within your upbringing has caused irreparable damage and differences with blood relatives. That's just the way life goes sometimes, but the beautiful thing is that you can create amazingly abundant friendships with those around you, tapping into mentors who become so close, understanding your unique psychology and demeanour so well, that they truly feel like part of your family.

I have never been one to have dozens of friends, I thought spreading out time with dozens of friends felt like a dissipation of energy. I enjoy quality over quantity with my friendships, and enjoy the highest charged energetic transactions in my friendships so that I know we are speaking from our true authenticity, as opposed to other interactions that may feel surface level or even superficial at times. I think with the adversity challenges I faced, I chose to attract from the universe the most meaningful and vital friendships that would allow me to thrive as a human being. You may have a similar circumstance, with little connection to your parents or siblings, but you chose to develop older mentors around you who provide nurturing qualities and create a powerful and very dear friendship, critical to anyone overcoming neglect and abandonment. You may have dealt with a particular type of sexual abuse and choose to surround yourself with people who convey personality characteristics of being very gentle, kind, and loving in character, so that a safety platform can be developed psychologically for you. Whatever your past is and the adversity you're carrying, I strongly and politely suggest that you build powerful and meaningful friendships around your inner niche, where you can truly be yourself and share your full expression of identity with that support system. Your friends and mentors will learn to thank you for being so honest, open, and brave in sharing what you've endured. This will help give you strength to overcome those psychological barriers so that you can continue to strive toward your path of ultimate happiness and living your ideal lifestyle.

I didn't realize how important my support system was to me until I was brought to my knees emotionally. For the last thirty years, I've been able to keep the walls up around my emotions. It was easy. I masked it with the most relentless and intense ambition I could have imagined, even at a young age, and I didn't take no for an answer in achieving my goals. I chased an ideal lifestyle of having the flexibility to be in charge of my time, and I read many self-development books, which I will get to, on how to become financially free and live the lifestyle of my dreams. I figured love was the easy part. Wow, was I wrong!

Once I started my first business—Time to Shine, a cleaning business—the universe started delivering me opportunities because I had put myself in the "zone" or "vortex" of being in the right place at the right time. My energy was very positive, ambitious, and patient, and more abundance organically flowed into my life. I had recently gotten out of a serious relationship with an amazing woman, which had seemed absolutely perfect. She was everything I could want in a woman—gorgeous, brilliant, sincere, wholesome, humanitarian, funny, loyal, dependable, accountable, honest, ambitious, athletic, and most importantly, she put up with my OCD and type A personality. She was substantially exceptional. What did I do when I wanted to really take the next step and visualize that it was absolutely possible to be successful in marriage, having a family and being a great husband? I ran for the hills, broke it off, and abandoned her. Little did I know that this circumstance would trigger something later on that would allow me to have the most important emotional breakthrough up to this point in time and change my life for the better. Survival mode can be a bitch.

Months later I became aware that this beautiful woman, whom I'd run away from because of my own fear of abandonment and subconscious survival mode mechanisms, was happily dating another man. I crumpled, and my heart felt like a piece of glass that had just shattered into thousands of tiny pieces. It was the most devastating point in my life in over twenty years, because I finally was vulnerable and emotionally exposed again! The protective emotional walls fell down, and I experienced the sensations of feeling human again, and it sent chills through my body. It took me back to a vividly painful memory of me as a little boy crying on the gravel road while walking home barefoot with nobody around and feeling deep, utter, excruciating pain. The only difference this time was that this boy was smiling at me, saying to my older, wiser self, "Jevon, you can have this piece of your heart back because you need it. Don't lose someone you love this much again; we want you emotionally complete for a human like this." It was the most empowering breakthrough I'd ever had in my life, something I wish for everyone who currently can admit that they have walls around their heart, only allowing the smallest circumstantial dosages of love into their fearful hearts, because having a fully functioning heart would just be too terrifying now, wouldn't it!? Once the walls fell, I began to truly believe in the next steps of happiness in my life of being a great husband and father and having a loving wife be the mother of my children. Nothing has ever been so vivid in my mind. Breakthroughs can be beautiful.

Through this breakthrough, I battled with building my confidence up for weeks after knowing that at the time what felt like the woman of my dreams was now with someone else. Those were some of the hardest days of my life. I needed my support system more than ever. I realized I had this new-found discovery of being more compassionate, kind, generous, and caring, and I could love unconditionally and not judge anyone's situation. I could finally feel love in my heart fully again. It was amazing, but I was still in deep, undeniable pain because this whole vulnerability thing was very new to me, and I felt like I wasn't invincible anymore. I felt like a human being finally. I'd come full circle in thirty years of existence to finally get my emotions back, to finally change my life, evolve, and adapt so that I could truly live my purpose of inspiring and helping people overcome adversity in their own lives.

The biggest challenge through this vulnerability was the psychological misconception that all the self-development and growth I'd done over the years, layering confidence on top of initiative, on top of perseverance, on top of relentless determination, on top of maintaining humility, and chasing success the way I do, was now gone. Was I starting from ground zero again, now that I was emotionally vulnerable, exposed, and could feel my heart beat again? It took me a few days to process the fact that I hadn't lost any of my personal growth or self-development I'd acquired and constructed intellectually, psychologically, and emotionally over the years. It was all there, stronger than ever.

I envisioned my own personal-growth Jevon Almond skyscraper of self-development. On each floor were layers of everything I had built—all my struggles, mistakes, triumphs, life lessons, attained wisdom, desire to be abundant, my beautiful niche of amazing people I'd built around me, the business I'd created with all the amazing customers and staff who helped contribute to our successful brand, my family, my health, my happiness, my perpetually optimistic perspective of life. It was all still there. On the top penthouse floor was an encasement with my heart, and the walls had fallen around it. I was back into a new transformed state of myself, so invigoratingly powerful that I want to share this story to let you know that your walls will fall down when the time is right. Perhaps we can even trigger your emotionally protective walls to fall while you read these words, opening you up to your most beautiful inner self, connecting you with who you were before the trauma you experienced, your true essence and infinitely powerful soul. That's what life is all about.

Before I had this epiphany and while enduring the pain and emotional vulnerability of the exploration process, I had moments of weakness, blurriness, numbness, and feeling like everything I had built up wasn't worth it if I couldn't be with who I loved. These were hard times, but there is light at the end of the tunnel. I began tapping into my support system, communicating with all my friends, telling them I needed their support. Me? Needing emotional support? Wow, I was in rough shape! I slowly started to embrace that I was finally emotionally complete and that it was normal to have moments of weakness in one's life. It's what makes living so dynamic and amazing. I connected more with my family and told more people I loved them in a short amount of time than I had in my entire life! I was onto something, and for the first time I was able to step into new, uncharted, vulnerable territory, finally feeling that my self-development, personal growth, and emotional completion was all in synergetic alignment. I found the last missing piece of myself, and my true purpose was to help people overcome adversity by leading, motivating, and inspiring them with my story, to increase their wellbeing and find purposeful fulfillment in life. We're going to find your purpose and unique ability as we continue to embark on this journey together. Your story is truly unique and incredibly special. Don't ever forget that.

CHAPTER 7

Parents Will Teach Anyway

"There are things in life that you have to work for,
and there are things in life you have to wait for."
—Anonymous

"When you're older, it will be harder to stay in shape, Jevon. You'll probably be overweight and unhealthy." My father spoke these words to me when I was young while I pummeled him with as many questions as I could in the shortest amount of time, trying to get the answers to life. My father is a very generous and loving man, always putting his kids first. I always admired him for this, but we'd lock horns over me wanting to be a very successful man, and him having this awkwardly frustrating perspective that you choose the "dark side" if you become successful. "You won't be able to afford nice things when you're older, Jevon." Things change. You have kids, get married and divorced, and take hard knocks. It took me years to understand what he was saying, while still choosing to agree to disagree.

I want to tell you something that may be hard to hear. If you want to be more successful than your parents in areas where you feel they struggled, you're going to have to learn to take their advice with a grain of salt. It's a very challenging thing to do at a young age. *You mean my mom and dad are wrong in what they say and how they encourage me?* That's absolutely a possibility. Just because it's advice from your parents or siblings doesn't mean you should follow it! I've lived a completely different way than I was raised, and I'm very grateful for it. If I chose to not seek mentors and just listened to my parents' advice, I would have set invisible limitations on how progressively awesome my life could one day become! It didn't mean it would be easy, though! When you're being raised, you're being raised in a family pattern created from the mindset of your how your parents were raised. Many times this builds a lifestyle trap that you have to become aware of as you become a teenager and mature into an adult. My father put it in my head at a young age that I "can't" get what I want in life. It was hard to swallow then, and it did delay my earlier development, but I'm now thankful for this advice because it's continued to motivate me to always pursue my goals and dreams in life.

I watched my dad over the years work so very hard, only to give it away to women in relationships who never seemed to have his best interests at heart. It was so emotionally deflating for me to watch as his son—everything he'd worked so hard for, in multiple situations, taken away while he just shrugged his shoulders and said

"That's life, Jevon." Well, it's not going to be my life, and it doesn't have to be yours either. That's the magic about taking advice from family. You can decide what you want to use! Isn't that an astonishing observation? Ultimately it comes down to your happiness and how you envision your life unfolding that is most important. If you feel advice from your parents will propel you closer toward your ultimate happiness and true life's purpose in an expedited matter, you may be right, but take it with a grain of salt, always.

The hidden lesson in what they tell you to do may actually be what you *don't* do.

As a child or teenager, it's hard to wrap your head around the idea that what your parents are teaching you at a certain moment in time may be what you're not to do in life. How many of us have heard our parents say things like, "Life isn't easy," "You'll get burned over and over," "You can't have everything you want in life," or "Stop dreaming and come back to reality". These may not feel detrimental to our psyche at the time, but as we develop into beautiful and aspiring human beings, they will limit the speed in which we grow over time. I want you to recognize that the life your parents envision for you may have a potentially negative impact on the life you envision for yourself, if you let it.

When I was younger, with my dad being a plumber by trade, it was a subconscious fall-back option to pursue his profession and make him proud. For some of us, this is a marvellous goal, following in the footsteps of our parents as doctors, nurses, engineers, lawyers, teachers, brain surgeons, plumbers, electricians, geologists, professional athletes, architects, or writers. If this truly makes you happy and is a burning passion for you, by all means, go for it! But for many, the illusion of following in the footsteps of our parents in terms of career and lifestyle can get us into big trouble when it comes to happiness and fulfillment if we aren't listening to our internal compass. Through personal growth and meditation, and reflection on what you really want in life, you'll find out what you're truly meant to do. Try to listen to the words people are using to describe what they think is best for you and your life. Use your spiritual intuition and wisdom. Are the words coming from a place of abundance, positivity, and true desire for your maximum fulfillment? Or are they a combination of their own lack of follow through on authentic purpose and fulfillment in their lives? Many people have lost or given up on their own dream and will tell you in all the ways they can, because of subconscious defeat, that you can't have yours. Let that sink in.

CHAPTER 8

Be the Sponge

"Watch your thoughts; they become words.
Watch your words; they become actions.
Watch your actions; they become habits.
Watch your habits; they become character.
Watch your character; it becomes your destiny."
—Frank Outlaw

I started off in my teenage life initially thinking I'd make the NHL. This was written in my Grade 6 yearbook. I was passionate about hockey and thought I was pretty good at it—enough to one day play professionally. Later in life, when I realized my hockey aspirations may not work out for me, I started to apply myself more in school, thinking I could one day be a dentist. This was short-lived, and then I started to really find my calling in real estate and entrepreneurial thought. It's funny how when we're younger, we bounce around many ideas of who we really want to be in life. Lawyers, doctors, engineers, teachers, scientists, professional athletes, celebrities, business owners—some kids are able to follow through on this well into their adult lives, living the very career they envisioned from the beginning. This is a very commendable thing to do, yet most of us have to play around with many ideas before one really resonates and takes us on our intended path.

I learned that I have a way of interacting with people, and I quite enjoy making them happy and feeling seen. I started in the homebuilding industry when I was eighteen, sweeping houses and cleaning up jobsites as a site assistant. It was a very humbling job for me, something I took very seriously, as I wanted to prove to myself that this was temporary but necessary for my development. I was already goal setting at a young age and knew, based on the books I'd already read (*The E Myth* by Michael Gerber; *Rich Dad Poor Dad*, *Cash Flow Quadrant*, and *Retire Young Retire Rich* by Robert Kiyosaki; and *Real Estate Riches* by Dolf De Roos) that it was just a matter of time before I got on the fast track of life and found out how to get out of this "rat race." I kept sweeping the floor of one of the beautiful homes that the current homebuilder I worked for was constructing, keeping my eye on the prize and having much patience. My focus at the time was to be the best damn site assistant the city had seen, as that was where I was presently at, making the most of what I was doing to the best of my abilities.

I met a friend who would open me up to the world of business at a young age and show me how to really groom myself to think like a young businessman. His name was Stephen, and although our friendship isn't as strong as it used to be due to the natural happenings of life, we will always have that friendship bond together. Around Stephen, I sponged up everything I could. He'd grown up around his mom and dad, who'd built a great business from the ground up, and he was now slowly being groomed to take over his family's business. I was a third-class welfare kid trying to learn how to make something of my life—two guys on opposite ends of the spectrum. We ended up working together, and he took on the role of essentially being the delegator, which I was happy for, as he didn't know at the time that my mission was to learn everything I could from him to reinvent myself and evolve one step closer to learning how to live a financially-free lifestyle. We became great friends over the next few years as I watched his mannerisms, the vocabulary he used, how he articulated his words when talking to people. I could tell we were raised much differently, and he was socially evolved and much farther ahead in the game than I was in terms of understanding business and economics. I admired his mindset, as it was entrepreneurial like mine.

I soaked it all up with humility and unstoppable determination, grateful for the opportunity for this kind of mentorship from someone who provided it unconditionally. I ended up evolving, taking myself slowly to the next level, stepping up my game, you could say. I was learning to become a businessman daily, thinking like the middle-upper class in terms of how to attain success and build a business that provides a product or service to a niche of customers, something that was very inspiring for me to consistently imagine. I always knew that I wanted to be a business owner. I just needed to acquire the tools slowly over time to finally execute that manifestation that was building inside of me over the years. I eventually ended up moving in with Stephen and his family for a few years while we started investing in real estate. I finally was taking the next steps in my development as a man, and it was awesome.

I will be forever grateful to have been taken in by such a lovely family, as they showed me what it took to make a house a home: hard work, patience, and unstoppable, unconditional love for one another. I sponged up the nurturing qualities from a family who was so generous and allowed me to feel like I was part of the family for a moment in my life, something I had missed out on as I lived in "survival mode" leading up to that point. This ability to be the sponge at an early point in life was vital in my development as a human being, learning how to be more confident, loving, caring, generous, thoughtful, determined, and patient while becoming a successful man in all areas of my life. I wish for you to be the sponge in your life, soaking up your surroundings and observing situations and happenings around you every day, with each one holding priceless lessons that will contribute to your development as a person.

As I fast-forward to my life now, in an evolved "sponge like" state of mind, I am incredibly observant, trying to learn from every situation I can in order to become more humble, philanthropic, thoughtful, generous, loving, kind, caring, and patient with my own desires, and to love people I know and don't know unconditionally. I've learned how to be kind to others in a consistent manner, as I've built myself up this way. It's possible for you to also always say hi to people at the coffee shop or grocery store, and always say thank you. It feels fantastic! Over the years, I've slowly built up my vocabulary just by learning what other people say and morphing that into my own style of words that are specific to my personality. I've transformed my personality and character to be professional and show polished etiquette when dealing with customers within our business and staff who are so kind and awesome enough to work for our brand, Time to Shine! Everything I do in life now is to make a positive impact on people's lives and give back to this world as much abundance as it has and continues to give me. This frame of mind can be built up for you too! It's closer than you think, and once you get on the path of evolving your state of mind to attract more abundance into your life, it will start to effortlessly flow to you and bring a smile to your face. Be the sponge; it pays off ten-fold over the duration of your life and is one of my most valued personality virtues. It can be yours too if you create it.

CHAPTER 9

Be Epic and Change Your Life

"When I stand before God at the end of my life, I would hope that I would not have a single bit of talent left, and could say, I used everything you gave me."
—Erma Bombeck

It was September 1, 2009, when I decided it was a good idea to go on an epic journey and ride road bikes with my dear friend Jim Bond from Penticton, British Columbia to the Mexican border. I had met Jim through my competitive endurance days. He's a professional triathlete and coach, and I looked up to him a lot when it came to my athletically competitive aspirations. He had done an epic trip bike touring in Europe, and this was a goal he had pre-planned to do solo. I asked if I could come, and he was like, "Sure, sounds fun!"

I had recently taken a few new home sales positions with two different homebuilding companies that didn't work out the way I'd envisioned, so I'd decided to take the plunge and become unemployed. It was very terrifying at twenty-five years old to be making the active choice to be unemployed, but it was exhilarating at the same time. I guess through all the books I'd been reading about starting a business, and learning how to expand the context of your mind to fit more content into it, I was getting closer to the end game of the "manifestation process" involved with launching a business. My perpetual goal-setting habits were finally starting to kick me in the ass, saying, "Now or never, Jevon. Time to take that risk you've been dreaming and writing about in your journal for over seven years." I desperately wanted to be an entrepreneur and was finally forcing myself into that uncharted "dare to be great" situation. I intrinsically knew that this trip would be the natural evolution process of me starting a business. I just didn't know what that business would be! It didn't matter. I was rolling with it and gearing up for the journey.

I wrote in a journal each day, recollecting our trip as we navigated our way south of British Columbia, through Washington state, then on to Oregon, and then onward to California. What a challenging but life-changing trip. We rode 3257 kilometres over twenty-seven days on bicycles. Pretty epic! The entire trip took me out of my comfort zone in the most dramatic fashion. We'd ride one-hundred-mile days like they were going out of style, for days without a shower, literally jumping into the ditch to camp once we reached a point of cumulative fatigue and it was getting too dark to ride. In my journal I described Washington state as "I don't know where I am; my body hurts and it has only just begun." Sounds pretty exciting, doesn't it?

As I continued to write each day about the terrain we were navigating, the torrential rain and smouldering-hot, desert-like weather conditions we faced, as well as the vicious head winds or cross winds, I noticed myself transitioning into being ready to start a business. At first I wanted to open up or purchase a Subway restaurant or a Booster Juice franchise, but I knew I'd need liquid capital to do this, and a large business loan to complete the modifications to the leased property in order to have a turnkey operation. What I didn't have was a lot of liquid cash, or a job to potentially be eligible to finance either of these ventures. The other option kicking around in my mind was to start a cleaning company.

During my younger years when I thought I was a hotshot selling homes, I decided to get a license plate for a silver BMW I'd been able to purchase through all my house sweeping days prior to transitioning to a sales career. It said TYM2SH9—Time to Shine. I always thought this was a pretty cool license plate, and it also came to me from aspirations to one day open up a chain of car washes. I thought to myself, *A cleaning company, huh Jevon? It would have to be a pretty good name for you to really build up substantial brand strength over the years and compete with the larger, reputable national conglomerates, as well as the franchises or locally owned Calgary-based organizations.* Then the light bulb came on and I realized that the name of my company was already predestined as "Time to Shine." It was a surreal moment for me as my manifestation process over the years delivered the name of the company I'd be using for the business I wanted to launch. Very epic indeed. They say that life begins at the end of your comfort zone. That is so true when it comes to taking risk in our own lives and living our true purpose. We have to be uncomfortable to promote change within ourselves, otherwise we'll stagnate and become complacent, a place I don't wish for you to be for any prolonged period in your life.

Once I had the idea in my head to launch the business, the true manifestation process from all my previous years of goal planning began happening right in front of me. When we reached the Mexican border, we had some champagne to celebrate the journey, packed up our bikes, caught a San Diego Chargers game, which was very entertaining, and then flew home. It was time to be an entrepreneur. I got home and immediately incorporated the business. I then got in touch with a very talented graphic designer named Christian Porter, who has become a great friend over the years. I was browsing various types of graphic design websites and gravitated toward his unique creativity. I articulated what I was looking for in terms of a very welcoming, sharp, dynamic, and professional looking corporate logo. He delivered a timeless logo for Time to Shine, a logo I knew would progressively carry more and more brand strength for each year we moved forward as an organization. It wasn't easy at the beginning, as I relentlessly pursued opportunities to grow our business, taking on maid services and homebuilder clients as we got our business model going. It's been amazing watching our brand grow from a few staff and a handful of clients to well over sixty staff and achieving triple digits for our corporate portfolio locations. I have goals to eventually become a nation-wide facility services company by aligning with nationally recognizable and reputable brands across Canada. This is a long-term vision, and it's been challenging but very exciting every step of the way.

Being epic is something I truly recommend for you in your own life. You may have debated running a half marathon or even a full one, doing an ironman, learning to play the piano or guitar, or taking flight lessons. You may be wanting to get on a plane to see Europe for the very first time, visit the coliseum or the Spanish steps, visit Venice, hike Kilimanjaro in east Africa, do a yoga retreat in Bali, Indonesia. You may want to climb Machu Picchu in Peru, scuba dive the Silfra Fissure in Iceland, touch two continental plates simultaneously, visit the pyramids of Egypt while riding by camel—whatever uniquely inspires you and has been on the back burner for far too long, do it! You'll find it incredibly rewarding and will gradually notice the dormant but very motivated part that was inside of you all along beginning to reveal itself to you, and that's when we start the beginning journey of living to our true potential.

CHAPTER 10

The Full Plate Misconception

"When in charge, ponder.
When in trouble, delegate.
When in doubt, mumble."
—Anonymous

When I was twenty-one, I thought that a full plate was the only way to be successful. I possessed an excessive amount of ambition and pure tenacity and wanted to fill up my plate to expedite the path toward becoming financially free and living the dream. I crammed as much into my schedule as mentally and physically possible for my own capabilities. I was working full-time for a homebuilder during the week, part-time at a night club on weekends, taking my real estate course and college degree part time in the evenings, trying to keep up a rigorous strength training routine at the gym, juggling a portfolio of approximately five properties, aspiring to start a business, and trying to be a great boyfriend to a wonderful woman I was dating at the time. Let's say this was an impossible juggling act, and when we overwhelm ourselves for too long, things start to fall off the plate slowly.

At that point in my life, I thought that by overwhelming myself, I'd expand the context of my mind and break through barriers into being able to accommodate a larger and larger workload. This can be possible for a certain period of time, which I think is best advised as a temporary approach to priority management. At this time, it was a rude awakening for me as my intimate relationship began to suffer slightly, one of the real estate deals went sideways, I began slowly struggling with a few of my part-time college classes, and I was beat down from lack of sleep, unable to adequately recover enough after hard workouts. I realized that my judgement and ability to apply the appropriate amount of energy into each of these priorities wasn't possible, no matter how much I tried to force it. I reached a momentary low at that point in my life, when it felt like I was being punished for my ambition, not knowingly acknowledging or grasping the wisdom that you can't force success. It has to happen organically through "patient ambition" (Chapter 11). I realized that in order to achieve any level of success, one needs to reflect on their own action. In John Maxwell's *The 15 Invaluable Laws Of Growth*, he quotes Peter F. Drucker: "Follow effective action with quiet reflection. From the quiet reflection will come even more effective action." This really resonated with me later in life as I realized that less is more when it comes to achieving your goals.

It took me a very long time to realize that one can thrive incredibly well with no more priorities than you can count on one hand. The five-finger rule is what I like to call it. One of your examples could be:

1. Family
2. Health
3. Career
4. Volunteer
5. Renovate the home

Where we tend to run into trouble is when we overwhelm our system with priorities such as:

1. Family
2. Health
3. Career
4. Coach your kid's hockey team
5. Renovate the home
6. Join a band
7. Write a book
8. Volunteer for a non-profit
9. Go after that degree you always wanted part-time
10. Start up that small business you've been aspiring to for years

While these are all incredibly commendable and exceptionally rewarding things to focus on, what we radically have to accept is that we're only one human being with limited time, resources, and energy. Sometimes we think we're superhuman, and for a short-term period of time these priorities may feel like they're actually being juggled efficiently and effectively. If we're going to be able to focus all of our energy on being the best we can be, I'd say it may be an enjoyable yet challenging exercise to see how full your plate really is and if you could hone your focus toward five primary priorities. You'll be pleasantly surprised with the amount of energy and focus you'll have with a narrowed down but enhanced focus on five or less major priorities.

My priority list would look like this, based on my current desired plate:

1. Family
2. Health
3. Managing existing businesses Breathe and Time To Shine
4. Teaching yoga
5. Completing *The Vulnerable Alpha*

I'd treat #4 and #5 as your revolving priorities that will change over a period of time, given whatever your commitments are at that point in your life. The top three key fundamentals create our own psychological equilibrium, and the other two are what we can adequately and optimally apply our energy and commitment toward simultaneously and be genuinely pleased with the results of our efforts.

CHAPTER 11

Patient Ambition

"Take a chance! All life is a chance. The man who goes farthest generally is the one who is willing to do and dare."
—Dale Carnegie

It's taken me many years to realize how important patience really is. When I was younger, I'd push and push and push with non-stop determination to achieve whatever goals I was working toward at that particular time. My ambition had an inexperienced youthfulness to it, which is what happens to younger people with an extraordinary amount of desire to succeed and achieve above average results. Patience is the last thing we think about when we're young, ambitious, full of endless energy and intensity, and essentially wanting to take over the world.

When I was about twenty-two years old, I was working very hard, or so I thought, on trying to break into the real estate industry. I worked tirelessly at building up my listing portfolio. This was a very hard thing to do at such a young age. I vividly remember doing listing presentations where I would get in the door with a prospective seller, make my pitch, and wait for them to say yes. I was oozing with the intense desire to succeed but lacking the detailed diligence and comfortable confidence that goes along with being a well polished salesman. We call this "desperate ambition." Anyone trying to succeed has to go through this phase, which is all part of the learning curve of increasing business acumen. The ambition is what keeps you hungry long after the desperation turns into exhaustion, and then patience is revealed.

Over the years I evolved as a businessman. When I took the plunge at twenty-five to start my own business, I really elevated the expectations of myself and wanting to succeed. I was listening more attentively to my prospects' needs, trying to be extremely detailed in how I created the tender proposal, keeping the interview process comfortable and professional, and throwing a few comments in to break the ice. I noticed a gradual shift in my underlying confidence, knowing quite accurately whether we had a strong probability of landing the acquisition or if there was an intuitive blockage that may be out of my control. This I attributed to having confidence in my sales and personality skills that had developed over the years. My calm confidence, patient ambition, detailed receptivity, and behavioural characteristics that were being relayed to my prospective clients, and the trust immediately heightened during our interaction, dramatically increased our chance to do business together. I truly believe that if your genuine concern is to do well for your clients, regardless of your business's market segment, you'll accelerate your growth in a very progressive timeline. I believe that money is simply an exchange of energy between two people. If you create a strong and trustworthy relationship with a prospect, they're most likely going to choose you over someone who could perhaps be offering less for their services, but it's all about the strong relationships and energy that will attract the loyal and amicable clients into your business model.

CHAPTER 12

Self-Time Sanctuary

"People get rich in their spare time, not at work."
—Robert Kiyosaki

I never really took self-time very seriously until my late twenties. What an amazing discovery in terms of relaxing into the success that you attract into your life from the universe. I started to prioritize self-time when I was able to create more free time for myself as an entrepreneur. I know that not everyone lives an entrepreneurial lifestyle, and I can appreciate that everyone has different obligations and responsibilities in life. I wish nothing more than for everyone to tap into their own unique version of self-time, because it's one of the hidden keys to finding your purpose and attracting infinite abundance and creation into one's life.

I kind of stumbled into this curiosity of self-time while reading a quote from Arnold Schwarzenegger: "Create a vision of who you want to be, and then live into that picture, as if it were already true." Wow, was that powerful stuff for me, knowing that he said that years before becoming a movie star. I read this while training quite heavily in 2008 for triathlon. In Calgary during the winter, you're forced to get a lot of your workouts done indoors. After my long and strenuous endurance workouts at my local YMCA, I started to habitually relax in the steam room for ten to fifteen minutes. I was physically relaxing, but my mind was churning one hundred miles per minute as usual. I decided right then and there to begin creating my vision and talking it out to myself if I was alone. If I was in the presence of other people, I'd silently create the vision of how I wanted my life to be.

The evolution of vision creation began, and I began to call it my "mental movie," talking out what was important to me at that particular time in life, reviewing my goals vocally with myself, and also talking about things that I wanted in my life but which I didn't yet possess. It was inspiring to do, verbalizing and visualizing the man I envisioned myself to be with the lifestyle I was living, even though it hadn't happened yet. I noticed my energy shift in terms of the confidence surrounding my goals, striving toward them as the potential of achieving them became easier, more relaxing, and enjoyable. I'd been writing in a journal for years, but this new "mental movie" manifestation started to really take shape and proved effective as well in my relationship goals, entrepreneurial goals, and athletic goals. What I talked about in my mind and envisioned repeatedly day after day was getting closer and closer to my reality. I was in a way "faking it until I make it."

Always Keep Growing, No Matter What

Years later and after more self-development, personal growth, and motivational books devoured, I had transformed myself again into a calmer, perpetually positive person who was really able catch myself if I let my conscious mind throw a negative thought my way, such as *You can't do that.* I'd take it in, feel it, and dismiss it right away. It takes time to do this, but it's very possible to do. You have to believe that the negative thought doesn't rule you and that you're in charge of how long it brews in your psyche! The shorter the better; you'll be far better off in terms of living, eating, sleeping, dreaming, and believing your inner optimism.

As humans, we don't start off with an abundance of positive thoughts; it's actually quite the opposite in a profound way. Our negative thoughts, such as cynicism, skepticism, pessimism, self doubt, laziness, self pity, self loathing, worry, sadness, lethargy, and procrastination, can generally overpopulate one's mental framework of how they operate and behave on a day-to-day basis. We have to re-train our mind, because it's very possible to be positive, confident, determined, tenacious, and basically a consistently happy and optimistic person. I know this sounds kind of fairy tale like and that it's not possible, but I can tell you that it really is. Napoleon Hill says it best: "Any idea, plan or purpose may be placed in the mind through repetition of thought." If you train your brain through goal setting, mental movies, and positive affirmations, your mental framework will start to shift and believe with confidence in what you're saying! I'd start with planning some short-term and long-term goals in your journal and then playing around with a sanctuary that works for you to begin acting out your own mental movie of what kind of lifestyle you envision yourself already living, even though you may not be there yet.

The past few years I've been implementing some exercises that have really helped fast-track maintaining a positive attitude, staying on track with my goals, and envisioning how my life is going to look when all my dreams start to begin coming true. I now utilize auto suggestion in a very big way, as well as the third way manifestation, provided by Gay Hendricks in his book *Conscious Living.* I also have adopted the sixth sense cabinet from the book *Think and Grow Rich* by Napoleon Hill, and I've customized my own mental movies by recording myself and playing them back for manifestation.

Auto Suggestion Implementation and Mr. Hendricks' "Third Way"

Auto suggestion is very simple in that you come up with a few key sentences about what you want to achieve in your life and then say them out loud, memorize them, and repeat daily with loud confidence. Strong breathing in between each auto suggestion statement helps strengthen subconscious delivery, in my opinion. You'd say something applicable to Mr. Hendricks' credo: "I commit to living in my zone of genius now and forever." This would be one desired proclamation out of many that you'd be constructing to deliver to yourself daily through verbal auto suggestion. It's addictive when you start to feel better about yourself and more in tune with your desires after a few days of consistently repeating the same auto suggestion over and over. The third way is pure magic, also inspired by Mr. Hendricks. With this, you add in the opportunities to absorb on a conscious and subconscious level the following for your auto suggestion exercise:

- I open to my full evolution and let go of any expectations I have for my life to be any particular way.
- I'm connected to infinite abundance and infinite creation.
- I achieve my goals by relaxing into the support that is around me all the time from the universe.
- I honour and appreciate the support that is around me all the time.

This is why Mr. Hendricks is one of my heroes, because he comes up with an abundance of magically enlightening gems in all of his books that one truly can't help but implement into their own personal growth arsenal. These would be in addition to the accumulated makeup of your daily auto suggestion. This will be a five-to-fifteen-minute exercise that will be, with all sincerity, a priceless practice for anyone to do consistently.

I want to take this even further and provide an example of my own combined mental movie and auto suggestion for your future practice of what you specifically want to attract in your life at any given time.

Auto Suggestion Exercise

I commit to living in my zone of genius now and forever.

I expand in abundance, success, love, and happiness every day as I inspire those around me to do the same.

I commit to discovering my upper limit behaviours (see The Big Leap by Gay Hendricks discussing the ULP problem) and having a good time, a great time, learning and conquering them.

I commit to building Time to Shine into a national facility services company by aligning with nationally recognized and reputable brands across Canada, once I have a stronghold in the Calgary and Edmonton markets.

No matter how hard it is, or how bad it gets, I'm going to make it (As Les Brown says, "You gotta be HUNNNNGRY!").

I commit to becoming the fittest I can athletically through yoga, cycling, hiking, running, swimming, strength training, hockey, tennis, and cross-country skiing, and the strongest I can be mentally through self-development, loving unconditionally, providing mentorship and seeking mentorship, being kind and grateful, being philanthropic and charitable, and always knowing the universe will deliver abundance if I'm sending it out first.

I commit to loving myself and loving those around me.

I commit to planning, preparing, and expecting to win athletically, financially, spiritually, emotionally, and entrepreneurially.

I commit to building Time to Help, and having The Vulnerable Alpha (Been saying this for years now!) written by myself, with the assistance of a future publishing company who can help with editing, distribution, and publicity management and with creating an audio book so that I can give back to those seeking mentorship and wanting to overcome adversity who can join my public speaking engagements and promotional book events. Whoa!

I open to my full evolution and let go of any expectations that my life has to unfold in any particular way.

I'm connected to infinite abundance and infinite creation.

I achieve my goals by relaxing into the support that is all around me, manifesting from the universe.

I honour and appreciate the support that is around me all the time. I show gratitude to the barista and the coffee shop, who patiently perfected my Americano. I'm grateful for the people who help me pay for my groceries, and others who meticulously stock the produce shelves so that I can buy the non-bruised, green Granny Smith apples! I'm grateful for the city crews who shovel the snow off the streets so I can go close business deals and do a yoga class without sliding off the road! I'm grateful for the utility workers, who allow me to use a fully operational furnace to stay warm, or provide me with that ever-so-important-these-days Wi-Fi signal in my own home, and I'm grateful for the flight attendants, the baggage handlers, air traffic controllers, and pilots who allow me to fly away on a beautiful jet plane to a tropical destination like Hawaii to live out my most ideal lifestyle. I'm so grateful.

I commit to staying open emotionally and trusting that the universe will deliver to me the love of my life when the time is right, and when we both are ready for each other. She's absolutely gorgeous, incredibly brilliant, kind, generous and wholesome, humanitarian, funny, and incredibly fit. She is charismatic, wise, magnetic, and inspires me every day to continue elevating myself as a man to become a better human being. When the time is right, I want her to be my wife and the mother of my children. I want to be her husband.

"She is a substantially exceptional specimen of human creation, and she's all mine." (I know I have my work cut out for me, don't I?).

Mental Movie Exercise

I wake up in Maui to my beautiful wife beside me, looking even more gorgeous than the first time I saw her, reflecting on how grateful I am to have her in my life. I hear the ocean waves crashing against the shore, and the birds chirping outside in the nearby bush as they do every Hawaii morning. I kiss her and tell her I love her. I get up and walk to our beautiful shower with full tile surround and thick ten millimetre glass, just the way I like it. I turn on the speaker system and listen to some chill tracks to get the therapeutic vibes going for my upcoming day. It's a big day. I finish my shower and walk to the kitchen and living room area, with picturesque views of the ocean right out my front window. There's an outdoor pool down on the walkout level, which I'll take a dip in later this evening. There's a light ocean breeze coming in, slightly massaging the palm trees leaves, waving them around very naturally. It's not the biggest ocean front property, because that doesn't matter, but it's on the ocean, and I earned and deserve every moment spent in this priceless sanctuary.

I blend up a beautiful shake with almond milk, almond butter, fresh mangoes, raspberries, strawberries, and a few scoops of Promasil protein powder, topped off with some organic plain yogurt. I make my coffee right around the same time, letting it cool off a bit while I drink my shake. It's a routine, and I love every minute of it. I sit down and think about my day. How are my businesses doing? How are all of our staff doing? Are they happy? Am I providing just the right amount of leadership? Are they inspired? How can I make my clients even happier with choosing us for their required services? At this point I own a few businesses, including Time to Shine and a chain of yoga studios, where I practise and occasionally teach at just for fun!

I'm working on another book, reflecting on how The Vulnerable Alpha went and how I can make my second book even more enticing and fulfilling for the audience who choose to read it. I'm also in the process of becoming the CEO of a let's say "Mergers and acquisitions wealth fund" for now (more details to come when appropriate), helping propel this mentors business model forward as much as I can, complementing the existing vision already created and ensuring longevity in the substantial success that is already established in the brand. I'm envisioning succession of the brand and grooming and polishing myself into the best man and leader possible so that I'm undeniably ready. This means merging and acquiring additional businesses in the future so that I can achieve my ultimate goal of a net worth of over 100 million dollars. I think about my speaking engagements booked for the year to promote The Vulnerable Alpha, trying to help my audience any way possible with overcoming adversity and tapping into their own inner resilience, which is so empowering to everyone involved!

I head to the garage and hop into our beautiful black Mercedes Benz SUV G Wagon, with tan caramel interior inside. I'm getting ready to head down to the beach for a jog with my wife. Although it's nice to have some nice things, the thought goes through my mind, as it always does, to remain humble and never let material belongings rule me or dictate a certain level of success. They're simply temporary belongings I can enjoy that certainly won't come with me when I die!

I glance at my Giant Revolt Pro Gravel bike and my Cannondale Scalpel SL modular 29er mountain bike in the other garage bay, waiting for me to ride later in the day. Perhaps I'll drive up to Kula and park near the Waipoli lavender farms, then climb my way up toward the top of Haleakala. Whoa, that's going to be a tough couple of hours this afternoon! I begin mentally salivating at the idea.

We drive to Baldwin Beach, where we head out for a walk together on the sand, feeling the ocean air hit us as we stare at the beautiful water. It's extremely blue today. Outstanding. We finish part of our beach stroll with a hand-holding cool down. This is paradise, and I've been asking the universe for this for many years, growing as a man to attract and bring this dream to fruition. It wasn't easy, and I never wanted easy, because this certainly was worth it.

We head back to the house, and she's going to head over to a late morning yoga class. Perfect—I can get my water bottles prepped for my ride with just the right electrolyte mix, and get my music jams ready for the epic climbing and island sweating to be had in less than an hour. I drive my way up to Kula and prep the bike for some uphill excitement. As I climb, I immediately start sweating, as I usually do when I start any type of exercise! I feel awesome and fit, appreciating all the previous years of fitness building that have allowed me to maintain my health and physique. I stop for a second as I'm climbing and have a look behind me at the dent I've put into my workout. This is achieved by staring back down to the west, overlooking Wailea and Kihei, unbelievably unobstructed up-country views of the ocean while I ride my bike. This is a dream, and I'm living it. I can see the Lahaina windmills, where I've hiked many times. I think I'll do that tomorrow!

I head back to the beach house and greet my wife again. She had a lovely yoga class and is now doing some work on her own business, reviewing her goals and wondering how she can be a better woman in all areas of life. Holy shit, am I a lucky man. But was it luck? (See "It's Not about Luck" later chapter!). We decide to head to Mambo Café tonight in Paia, a pretty chill place for dinner. We're going to have chicken fajitas and enjoy a few Mai Tais. The fresh pineapple is delicious! We head back home and I read to her what I've been working on, asking her opinion. We make love and it's magnificent. Where I've come from and where I am now, the juice was worth the squeeze.

I hope this gives an example of how vivid I want you to envision and create your mental movie. Dream big, make it so real that you salivate for it, smile at the thought of living that life. It is possible, and you deserve it. Do it every day you can, auto suggestion and mental movie. I've recorded many mental movies over the years, changing where I'm waking up occasionally, depending on my mood. Sometimes it's in Calgary or Canmore, other times it's in Maui or Mallorca, Spain. Wherever it is, be specific and continuously ask for it from the universe, because trust me, it's listening! Try to be consistent with your auto suggestion. I've been saying them out loud to myself for years, customizing as I go or adding in new commitments to my future lifestyle and aspirations.

Napoleon Hill's Sixth Sense Exercise

The next exercise is the sixth sense cabinet, inspired by Napoleon Hill in his book *Think and Grow Rich*. You're essentially drawing a rectangular "boardroom" on a piece of paper with your name in the top with a circle around it. This is your first name bubble. You begin to add in who else will be sitting in your desired boardroom "cabinet" meeting. Envision what mentors you'd have beside you, in exact order, and plan accordingly as to how large you want your boardroom to be. My boardroom would consist of mentors of mine such as Gay Hendricks, John Maxwell, Robert Kiyosaki, Tony Robbins, Coco Chanel, Oprah, Zig Ziglar, Napoleon Hill, Donald Trump, Howard Schultz, Jim Treliving, Lance Armstrong, Warren Buffet, Orville and Wilbur Wright, and Magic Johnson. Your mentors are specific to you and what inspires you in your life, and the direction you want to go in order to achieve your dreams.

Now the fun part is asking what the question will be for that particular boardroom meeting. You may ask: How can I achieve my ideal lifestyle? How do I attract my life partner? How do I achieve greatness in my life? How can I become an entrepreneur? How do I become financially free? The results will be creatively mind-blowing. This is all about tapping into our imagination and letting the universe organically manifest advice from mentors we seek it from but aren't able to have physically in our presence. What an empowering exercise. Enjoy!

CHAPTER 13

Be Humble Early

"Principle One. Don't criticize, condemn, or complain."
—Dale Carnegie, *How to Win Friends and Influence People*

Humility is such a beautiful thing, one of the best virtues a human being could possess. Maintaining it is a constant struggle as we progress in life toward our goals and dreams, dealing with all the triumphs and failures that come along with it. Coming from my background, appreciating life and all it has to offer was easy for me at the beginning. As I continued in life to grow and want to increase my level of success and abundance, get out of the rat race and live my ideal lifestyle, I realized it was going to be something to consistently put emphasis on maintaining and enhancing.

Recognizing the Gratitude Grinch

As you begin to bring more success and abundance into your life, the invisible "gratitude Grinch" begins to challenge your subconscious mind. "You worked hard for this and you deserve it." This is a valid and appropriate comment, but we run into trouble when we begin to feel deserving of more and more things in life, and the "gratitude Grinch" temporarily steals our gratitude and appreciation for all that we've built our lives up to be in such an abundant fashion. Slowing down and appreciating how good life really is, and how far you've come, sometimes can be forgotten in the midst of a momentary "humility" imbalance. If left uncorrected, it can begin to manifest potential behavioural patterns that you may resent after some "self-time" meditation.

I've sometimes caught myself not expressing gratitude for smaller things in life as more abundance comes into it. The beautiful part about it is that you can create "catch mechanisms" to recognize and correct this kind of behaviour immediately. I can be guilty of this when the conversation doesn't go the way I initially had envisioned with my phone provider, a government representative, someone booking a flight for me, or a utility representative. I catch myself perhaps being rude, or short, or trying to control the situation, not expressing gratitude but also letting a smaller situation become bigger in my mind than it has to be, challenging my humility. We all deal with these kinds of negligible circumstances with people throughout our day-to-day routines, and I find that being kind and patient in these small interactions makes a dramatic difference in maintaining our humility and gratitude. Just remember, if you think you're a big fish, it's probably a small pond. Having that mentality helps me check my ego at the door as I strive toward more abundance in life. This is why I believe philanthropy and charitable giving are such important components in anyone's life who wants to really have an abundant equilibrium with the universe.

Give Back ASAP

In the early years of being engulfed in my first business, Time to Shine, I was focused on building the business and managing all of our customers' needs and wants (which never stop being important!). With consistently keeping our staff happy and handling all the behind-the-scenes licensing, permits, insurance, government, and accounting obligations, the last thing I allowed myself to have time for was giving back. When I actively made giving back to organizations a priority for my business model, abundance increased exponentially in my life, not just my business. I started small, supporting the Calgary Women's emergency shelter with their annual charity galas and arranging charitable donation arrangements with Big Brothers/ Big Sisters of Calgary, the Ronald McDonald House of Calgary, the Daraja Foundation, as well as the Women's Centre of Calgary. It doesn't matter what amount you start at, the key is committing to support a foundation and executing on that promise. The floodgates of abundance and positivity flow into your life when you can finally own the idea inside yourself that giving back is a fundamental part of your day-to-day life. Start small, giving your time and any financial resources you can that are affordable with your current lifestyle, and don't look back on the momentum of being a philanthropic human being.

Create Your Own Humility Experiment

Still gathering the necessary tools I needed to mentally be ready to take the leap and become an entrepreneur, I wanted to get back to the basics of humility. I challenge you as your friend in this universe to think of what would bring you back to your basics of humility. It could be volunteering your time, giving some things away that are important to you, as you know the recipient will be eternally grateful, or taking on a job that will undoubtedly bring you back to your roots of humility. In your circumstance, you may feel the desire to be a better person, or you may have hit a wall with trying to attract more abundance into your life. This is the way to fast track attracting abundance from the universe. For me it was picking up paper routes, delivering three hundred papers in the morning, seven days a week for half a year. I didn't have to take on this second job, for my financial circumstances were not in dire straits, but I wanted to challenge myself to sink deeper into the feeling of humility. I'd pick up my papers every morning around 2:00 a.m. during the week, and 4:00 a.m. on weekends, and deliver papers to doorsteps for about three hours. The duration of my paper delivery days also coincided with one of the coldest winters Calgary had seen in years, as I vividly remember the temperature with the wind-chill being -50 for almost a week straight.

I analyzed and observed my surroundings, picking up on my thoughts that would come in and challenge my fundamentals. *Why are you doing this, Jevon? Isn't this going backwards? You want to build a business and now we're delivering papers in the freezing cold, seven days per week? What the hell is the matter with you? Have you lost it?* My girlfriend at the time understood why I was doing it, as she always knew that my methods of personal growth and self-development were prone to being unorthodox. Some of my friends understood why I was doing it; acquaintances who became aware that this was a second job for me were perplexed and asked me why I was doing it. I'd explain that it was all part of the plan and what I needed to do to acquire the mental tools to maintain my humility as I acquired tremendous success in the future. It was the calm of humility before I embarked on the relentless journey of pursuing my most ideal lifestyle and living out my true purpose in life.

CHAPTER 14

Stay True to Your Own Vision

"Be true to your vision, and your
vision will be true to you"
—JKA

While pursuing your dreams and trying to mentally manifest the life you want to live, there will be distractions along the way. You'll have to recognize these distractions and stay true to your own vision. It will all be a test to see how badly you want to live your ideal lifestyle and find out why you are here, to find your true purpose in life.

Does This Decision Maintain the Pursuit of My Highest Level of Harmonized Equilibrium?

We've all made decisions that we knew weren't the right ones for us, and we even had warning signs, or "red flags," that this just doesn't feel right. *Don't take that job. Don't date that person, they're bad news. You two aren't meant to be together. I've got a feeling in my gut that I should give this decision more thought.* We've all been there, feeling intuitively that certain decisions should be thought out more before acting on them. Then our developed spheres of influence, or "niche," also have an opinion on where we're heading in life, vocalizing their advice and recommendations as if they were living out our lives through their own eyes. This advice is important, coming both from your internal intuition and your external niche, who have come to know you quite well and understand with a variable amount of accuracy (depending how close you are to your niche) how you tick emotionally and psychologically. The trick is to know yourself, and this is no easy task.

It takes years of development and training your mind to catch when you may not be at your best to make sound decisions for your future emotionally, spiritually, and financially. Over the recent years I've been able to recognize when an opportunity shows up to challenge your authentic loyalty to your own vision. It could be someone you met with whom you know you don't align long-term, yet you begin moving down the path of getting to know each other and becoming intimate. The next thing you know, you're in a serious relationship with someone who isn't meant for you! We've all been there, haven't we? We've all been broken, or broken the hearts of other people, leading them down the road of ruin, knowing that deep down we aren't following our own path toward ultimate happiness. Other relationships we inevitably become victims to, crumpling us emotionally, bringing us to what feels like an emotionally crippling breaking point.

It isn't until we slowly heal, by eliminating any destructive behaviours and focusing on positive lifestyle choices, that we realize there were embedded lessons in this relationship experience that were life-changing emotionally, spiritually and improved our outlook on life, taking us further into the depths of living our ideal life, with an open heart full of love.

Recognizing When Your Mind Wants to Overwhelm You

I've been tested along the way with limited time and energy clashing with my perpetually abundant entrepreneurial desires, and at times this significantly hindered my ability to have a concentrated focus toward primary goals. When things were progressing steadily with Time to Shine, our client list slowly becoming larger and more qualified, loyal staff being referred to our business from existing staff members, I could have continued focusing solely on the business model that was providing abundance in a very progressive way. However, for a young, relentlessly ambitious mind, this is never enough, so exploration on additional opportunities and ideas continued to flow.

One beautiful afternoon while riding my bike for a long ride south of Calgary near Spruce Meadows, where I'd come up with some of my best ideas, another large one showed up and began demanding my attention and energy. The idea was to create a one-stop-shop corporate service conglomerate made up of service offerings such as commercial property management, residential rental property advertisement, landscaping, security monitoring, corporate recycling and document shredding, and of course what we were already doing, corporate commercial cleaning. I incorporated the "Time to Group," "Time to Rent," "Time to Lease," and "Time to Landscape," and a corporate conglomerate manifest was born. It didn't stop there, as I started to envision all types of businesses that could form part of the "Time to Group." The opportunities were endless, and I had to get a grip on reality, available time, and the resources I had to execute this magnificently overwhelming vision. It took me a few years to realize that the "full plate concept" and "patient ambition" were lessons talking in my ear at the time, as I continued to dream of how I was going to take a deeper plunge entrepreneurially and never look back on carrying out the conglomerate aspirations.

I took a deep breath many times throughout many days and realized finally that I had to stay true to my vision by setting realistic expectations on my entrepreneurial ambitions. Unless we were of the rare privilege to be raised around incredible people who started some of the most successful businesses in the world, like Google, Facebook, Twitter, Amazon, and many others, we have to understand and appreciate that we have limited resources and time available to us as we take steps toward achieving our desired vision. I quickly realized that I needed to first turn the business I was currently immersed in into an even more successful model, one that could eventually be grown and maintained without my involvement. Robert Kiyosaki says it best: "A true business is one you can walk way from for a year, and come back to see it more profitable, and more optimally ran than when you left." A challenging yet powerfully true statement coming from a very successful man. He is so accurate in that we really do need to apply this in our own lives when it comes to achieving our goals. The last thing we want to do is spread our vision and resources too thin, weakening our ability to carry out what we sought to achieve in the first place.

Should I really buy this business in a completely different geographical area right now? Why do I want to buy this coffee shop franchise so badly? Will this decision distract me from my vision or expedite the curve of progression in achieving it sooner? Recognize your "full plate" and don't ever let go of your relentless desire to succeed and achieve your goals, but be realistic to the "timed release" of your energy and commitment to each goal as life progresses. This isn't about procrastination; this is about maintaining psychological, emotional, and spiritual equilibrium while chasing your dreams.

CHAPTER 15

Everyone Wants You to Fail

"Success is often achieved by those who
don't know that failure is inevitable."
—Coco Chanel

This chapter was very enticing to visualize how I would put down the right words on paper and provide a resoundingly positive impact regardless of the title. Isn't life structured this way? Daring to dream is "risky" and "unlikely." People will say you "can't" do that. "Wilbur and Orville Wright are trying to fly a plane, that will definitely be an epic fail, imagine what their family is going through." We need to embrace and love the idea that we'll have to endure painfully humbling experiences, validating internally that failure is an inevitable ingredient in one shape or form, required along our pursuits until we break through to achieving undeniable success in our own lives.

Smash through the Limitations of Your Temporary Failure

I was in my first year as a business owner in the residential and commercial cleaning sector, learning and experiencing all that being a small business owner entails. I'd recently left the new home sales sector, just finished an epic life-changing bike trip to Mexico with a great friend, and was now full throttle toward achieving success in my first business. Being a small business owner isn't easy, and the beginning steps are very hard and overwhelming, as there are so many things to put in place before your business can actually grow!

I had just incorporated our company federally and provincially; collaborated with a graphic designer to create our beautiful logo; arranged our WCB, liability insurance, and bond requirements to do business; had a website built; ordered our business cards; and was off to the races, determined to acquire our first piece of business. I reached out to my network of people I knew, ambitious to promote our business and the vision I wanted to uphold. The focus would be on relentless customer service, great quality, and budget alignment for every customer we had the pleasure of doing business with. Flurries of phone calls were being made, seeds were being planted, irons were being put in the fire, and I knew it was a matter of time before the business would grow. *I can make this work. You can succeed, Jevon! Keep going!*

For the first few months, which felt like an eternity, little business was streaming in. We were landing some maid services clients, which were mostly people within my niche whom I'd gotten to know through my years in new home sales, and some micro commercial clients who brought in revenue similar to a maid service's client on a bi-weekly schedule. I was happy to do some of the cleaning myself at the beginning, helping lead the way in getting my hands dirty, embracing the humility once again of being a business owner starting from the ground up. I helped where I could, being involved with my general manager at the time, while we began to train our first staff members, instilling the quality and customer service expectations that we still maintain today at Time to Shine with great pride. We were taking very small bites in the market share we wanted to enter into, and I was appreciating to the fullest depth that you don't become a multimillion-dollar company overnight. It just takes time.

At the time I felt as though my own ambitions had limitations and that I was "failing" on expedited growth. I had to realize that it takes time to reap the rewards of the harvest from the seeds you plant. I was putting hundreds of irons in the fire, cold calling and prospecting door to door, the mentality of "faking it until I make it" never being more applicable, which every small business owner can relate to. It's the feeling that takes over as a business owner, knowing you're over your head but so focused and determined to gain that client's business that the confidence you exude in your brand and the willingness to succeed wins the contract. Wow, having customers choose us feels good! What an amazing feeling in business, and the desire to replicate it only increases with every yes, savouring the word after knowing how many hundreds or thousands of prospective responses had been "no" along the way.

It began to get easier, like the universe started rewarding me with abundance for the momentum I was creating with my ambition and sharp focus on succeeding in the sector I'd broken into. It was intoxicating, downright addicting to beat out other competitors in the RFP (Request for Proposal) or "tendering process." There's nothing more satisfying than building your brand from the ground level up, strengthening your corporate culture, attracting the right staff, earning a solid reputation, and being in the zone as a business owner where prospective customers gravitate toward you. It is possible, and it's a priceless feeling, one I want for you as we continue to pursue achieving our own unique dreams together!

Don't Be Afraid to Lead the Way with Your Family and Niche

You may find that once you get on your "path of no return" toward infinite abundance and creation in your own life, others who previously may have subconsciously thought you "can't" do something, or would "fail" at it, now become your biggest fans. The remarkable thing is you know that continuing your pursuit of your own goals and lifestyle aspirations increases the inspiration and motivation in the lives of those around you. What an amazing thing! Perhaps your father, who told you that you're out of your mind to start a business ("You'll get eaten alive.") now finally sees what you're made of, and you even surprised him beyond his wildest dreams. Maybe it's a sibling who doubted you right up to the point of breakthrough. Just because those around us may unknowingly "want" us to fail, it's not because they're bad people; it's quite the contrary. As humans, we're wired to predominantly be held hostage by our negative thoughts, temporarily restricting us from being successful as we march down the road of uncertainty with a smile on our face because success awaits us!

Inspire those around you and within your niche, be it family or friends. Initially they may not want you to succeed, due to the fear that your life will dramatically change, causing your relationships to be altered. Those who love us will be temporarily confused about wanting us to fail, mainly out of fear of us becoming someone they haven't met yet, someone who's vocalized inspiration challenges others to look in the mirror to make sure they're living out the pursuit of their dreams. Many of us are yet to meet the beautiful person we're destined to become, and once we go confidently in the direction of our dreams, that ultimate person is revealed and we begin living our true purpose and feeling more happiness and love than we ever thought was possible.

CHAPTER 16

Mentors Are Everywhere

"Often people attempt to live their lives backwards; they try to have more things, or more money, in order to do more of what they want, so they will be happier. The way it actually works is in reverse. You must first be who you really are, then do what you need to do, in order to have what you want."
—Margaret Young

When I picked up the *E-Myth* by Michael Gerber in my mid-teens at the local bookstore, it was such a good feeling knowing that it might be possible that some of my curiosities in life thus far could be answered by reading other people's words. At that time, learning about the technician, the manager, and the entrepreneur was all fascinating to absorb as my eyes scanned through the words, relaying them to my mind. I initially started out reading business and real estate books, not knowing that this would take me on a never-ending pursuit of learning more about successful people's opinions, taking pieces of their perspectives on life, growth, abundance, and success and then applying it in my own life. Picking a book to read was like being able to select the virtual school you attended, and also having the ability to select who your "mentor" would be for a certain snapshot in time. Books have guided me at times of critical growth curves in life, vulnerable circumstances where you feel you need deeper answers than what you're currently able to find internally, or externally through your niche and perceived surroundings.

Find the Mentors Who Pertain to Your Desires

Everyone's desires in life will be different; that's what makes this world so unique. When we're at our optimal levels of lifestyle equilibrium, we can truly feel blessed in the ability to pursue all the answers we seek to the most important questions coming from our own authentic minds. If you're an aspiring athlete, seek mentors who have made it in the field you desire to be successful in. If you want to be a musician, study and emulate all musicians whom you admire, respect, and envy for the lifestyle they live and achievements they've earned. Begin devouring books that they've written, quotes that are important to them and convey who they are as people, how their minds operate, and what behavioural patterns set them apart from others in their professional field. Treat yourself as their apprentice and live eat, sleep, and breathe the way they do so you can fully understand what it takes to elevate yourself to a similar level. Once you feel like you've increased the mental frequency in which you're residing when it comes to pursuing the dreams specific to you, absorb the lessons from mimicking this mentor and intertwine them with a customized approach to your own personality and character development. The way you behave compared to your mentor will never be in flawless alignment, nor should it be. When studying various mentors throughout my life, they gave me keys to different vaults inside myself, opening up new areas of growth and opportunity, an alternate perspective on how to achieve my desired goals. Robert Kiyosaki was a pivotal mentor for me in my younger years of development, and still is to this day. I find myself re-reading many of his books that I read in my teens, pulling out the same lessons he taught me years ago and then re-applying them in my life now. Your mentors will also teach you different things at various stages in your life; it's quite remarkable to know that they can have an evolutionary impact on your prolonged personal growth, providing never-ending longevity when it comes to self-development.

I've been an aspiring athlete in the past as well, wanting to pursue the professional cycling dream, riding in a pro tour peloton and navigating the European landscapes while watching fans scream as I suffered the depths of my athletic limitations. Athletes like Lance Armstrong, Mark Cavendish, and Bradley Wiggins became admirable mentors for me at that stage of life as I read through their books *It's Not about the Bike*, *Boy Racer*, and *In Pursuit of Glory*, all autobiographies detailing how each athlete ticks on a psychological, intellectual, and emotional level. I'd soak up whatever gems of wisdom they could offer, mistakes they made that I could potentially avoid, and opportunities for growth I could tap into personally after each mentor relayed areas they missed out on in terms of maximizing potential. Every mentor you study provides a priceless opportunity to expedite your curve of progression toward achieving your dreams. This is of the utmost importance in life, as we only have limited time on this earth.

While I aspired to be a professional athlete, my business goals and dreams, as well as personal growth desires, were never put on the back burner, as I always had the thought of pushing toward all my biggest goals in life simultaneously, with equilibrium. Throughout the years of my development, the major mentors who stood out for me and continue to are:

1) Robert Kiyosaki. Recommended reads within his *Rich Dad Poor Dad* series would be the *Cashflow Quadrant*, *Rich Dad Poor Dad*, and *Retire Young, Retire Rich.* This man changed my life when it came to thinking like a businessman and learning about how people in different quadrants—whether it be the employee, self-employed, business owner, or investor—all think differently. In order to get out of the rat race, one needs to recognize where they currently reside and how to acquire the mentality to move into the desired quadrants that provide the most opportunity, freedom—namely the business and investor quadrants. If you are a parent, consider getting this for your children, they will thank you years later for it.

2) Gay Hendricks. Recommended reads of his are *The Big Leap* and *Living Consciously*. He has many books within his series, all of tremendous value, but to me the book that possessed monumental principles that could immediately be applied to my life was *The Big Leap*. We reside in four zones: the zone of incompetency, the zone of competency, the zone of success, and the zone we all want to be in—the zone of genius. From him, I learned how to break through different zones, validating what may be causing me to "upper limit," which is a nice way of saying I'm holding myself back big time because of various circumstances. He shows priceless wisdom in recognizing the "Third Way" universal manifestation principle, as well as giving you the tools to articulate your own "unique ability," helping you gain a better understanding of your purpose in life. This man is an exceptional example of a human being living to his true potential, in his zone of genius, at his highest frequency, continuing to break through previously conceived ceilings of maximum growth, as one recognizes the ceiling is only that, a temporary barrier.
3) Bill Rancic. A recommended read of Bill's would be *You're Hired*, which he wrote after being selected as the "apprentice" from Donald Trump's hit TV show *The Apprentice*. What a magnetic, electric, and charismatic person, whom I had the pleasure of meeting at one of his public speaking book promotion events for entrepreneurs in my

home town of Calgary, Alberta. Bill proved that you don't have to come from a Harvard education to make a long-lasting successful impression in life. One of his first businesses, Cigars around the World, started with the most humble beginnings and grew into something much bigger, surpassing levels of success he had envisioned for himself, demonstrating what it's like to be living out your dreams and the universe rewarding you with new, extraordinary versions of yourself you didn't know were previously possible.

4) John Maxwell. The recommended read for John would be *The 15 Invaluable Laws of Growth*, a gem I still refer to quite frequently, challenging myself with what law of growth I'm currently struggling with or running into resistance with. This man is very talented at inspiring others, having a place for all the wisdom he absorbs so that it's easily accessible, and pushing the limits of growth with perpetual consistency.
5) Napoleon Hill. The recommended book here would be *Think and Grow Rich.* Such a powerfully magnificent book in terms of attracting riches into your life and realizing the word "rich" has very little to do with money and everything to do with abundant thinking, while the universe listens. His sixth sense cabinet exercise is true genius, as well as touching on the fundamentals around attracting your desires in this world and making them so vivid in your mind that your dreams already "feel" like they're in your possession.

6) Jen Sincero. I'd recommend reading *You Are a Bad Ass*. It's hilarious in that the concepts Jen talks about hit hard at home but make you laugh your ass off while reading it. She's a uniquely talented author in that her inspirational wisdom leaves an imprint on you through constructive thought, and her perplexingly entertaining humor makes you burst out laughing while simultaneously feeling euphoric because she helped you discover your own personal epiphany specific to your life.
7) Michael A. Singer. A strongly recommended read of Michael's would be *The Untethered Soul*, an intellectually stimulating masterpiece on understanding your consciousness and learning to control how your mind reacts to things internally and externally based on your surroundings He demonstrates that with the highest level of self-discovery, one can master their own mental fortitude, only focusing on their true purpose in life, and keeping the mind strong and heart open as we chase our dreams and understand our destiny. Picture a vehicle and a driver, your body being the vehicle, your mind being the driver, and your soul is in the back seat watching the journey. Profound.
8) Donald Trump. I know he's a public icon, and people hold strong opinions of him as a person, but I know that this guy knows his stuff when it comes to business and real estate. The recommended read that I always fall back on is *The Way to the Top*. It has little to do with

advice from Donald and more to do with success advice from some of the most successful people he's interacted with over the years, including their wisdom on achieving your dreams. Very inspiring and humbling to dive into this read and immediately draw motivation and firm direction on your path to success.

CHAPTER 17

It Has Nothing to Do with Luck

"A man on top of the mountain didn't just fall there."
—Vince Lombardi

We've all witnessed people achieving remarkable accomplishments in their lives. "She started her own business and it took off so quickly." "He decided to start painting pieces of art, and now his pieces are displayed throughout some major hotel chains and art galleries all over the world!" "She quit her job and decided to write that book she always dreamed of, and now it's on the shelves at my local book store, and she's hosting speaking engagements around the world to promote her book!" An auto response that usually comes to mind is "You're/they're so lucky" that it just came together like that. It doesn't work like that for everyone. I believe there is truth in that statement to a certain extent, but if you really understand your purpose in life, the potential outcome of failure should never stop you from pursuing your purpose. As Napoleon Hill says: "Take a chance! All life is a chance. The man who goes farthest is generally the one who is willing to do and dare." How beautiful of a feeling to know you're living your dreams, and others have no other response but to tell you that "you're lucky." I want to put emphasis on the idea and possibility that when phenomenal things begin to happen in someone's life, it has nothing to do with luck and everything to do with manifesting from the universe the abundance they want to attract into their lives.

Right Place, Right Time

I believe that being in the "right place at the right time" has a lot to do with synchronicity in that it was a "meaningful coincidence" that created the circumstance a particular person is now suddenly and miraculously living out in the present. I find that it's far more powerful and inspiring to be genuinely happy with a huge smile when I hear about or personally witness a success story through someone I know. I can personally attest to the magic our minds can hold when applying energy toward certain things you want to attract in this life: feeling them, believing they're possible, and then trusting in the universe to deliver them. And lo and behold, they slowly start to appear. It's about elevating your frequency constantly to make sure that your complete being is aligned with your desires. Once this is happening and you're doing everything humanly possible to attract what you want in this life from universal intelligence, I promise you it begins to listen.

I had the unique pleasure of knowing singer and songwriter Kiesza before she became a famous pop star. She came out with the hit song "Hideaway" and to many became an "instant" star. Watching her perform on *Jimmy Kimmel* was truly inspiring, and I was awe struck watching someone living to her true potential. What impressed me even more was where she started, playing at the local Ship and Anchor pub in Calgary, Alberta, and even before that doing solo performances at local community centres, polishing her talent and slowly taking the necessary steps to one day be living her dream. Now she's a superstar, and I couldn't be happier for her! We all need to get up off our butts and start putting the pieces in place to recognize our potential, discover our purpose, and begin the relentless pursuit, because that's what life is all about!

Create Your Own Luck with Persistency

There's a quote that resonates with me with respect to persistency that says the following:

> Nothing in the world can take the place of persistence. Talent will not' nothing is more common than unsuccessful men with great talent. Genius will not: unrewarded genius is almost a proverb. Education will not: the world is full of educated derelicts. Persistence and determination alone are omnipotent.
>
> —Calvin Coolidge

I believe this holds true with respect to how powerful persistency really is. It creates luck for you. If you don't believe me, look at the dreams you want to achieve in your life and start living them out now. As you've been reading through this book, planning your goals, carrying out your auto suggestion, practising your sixth sense cabinet of advisors, as well as creating your mental movies during your self time, take all of these things and deeply apply all the persistency toward attaining the goals you have for yourself right now. Start with actively making baby steps each day that will inevitably lead to more opportunities opening up so that you can work toward achieving your vision in a more progressive way. It is real, and it can work like magic as long as you have faith that it's possible, and that feeling is more powerful than the fear of it not happening.

CHAPTER 18

Lifestyle First

"If you can conquer your own self-doubt and laziness, you will unlock the door to your true potential."
—John Maxwell *The 15 Invaluable Laws Of Growth*

Travel for six weeks? What about my job, my career? Where would I go for that long before missing home? My boss would never allow it, and imagine the debt I'd accumulate on a trip that long.

We've all heard this before from people we know when talking about travelling and getting away on a vacation. During the fall of 2010, shortly after starting my first business, I remember vividly talking with a co-worker I was selling homes with about an upcoming vacation I planned to book. It was to Hawaii with who would eventually become one of my best friends, Patrick. I hadn't really known Patrick very long prior to our trip, as we'd only met at a bike race earlier in the summer and very casually talked about perhaps doing an epic bike training camp somewhere tropical. I hadn't chatted with him in months, and then he called me up and asked if I was going. It was for two weeks, and although requesting the time off in advance with my co-worker, he was having none of it. He justified the recommendation of me shortening my trip by a week by saying that I was already very spoiled as a contractor when it came to travelling for bike races, and he was right. I was getting used to taking a three-day weekend here, or a four-day weekend there, to go pursue my competitive racing aspirations, and it was a lifestyle I planned on continuing and only making better.

At first I explained to Pat that unfortunately it was just too much time off for me and would really disrupt my current home selling initiatives with my sales colleague. I remember sitting in the show home after hanging up the phone, wondering if that was the correct decision right then and there. It was at a pivotal yet very uncomfortable moment for me because with my business, I wasn't yet set up to sustainably cover my monetary obligations, such as vehicle, mortgage, cell phone, groceries, and not to mention a two-week trip to Maui to ride my bike and relax on the beach. The part-time, flexible new home sales job was quite a sweet scenario for me while I ambitiously planned to push my business to the next level and continue with fitness and travel goals.

I decided that this was going to be my mountain to climb and make a life-changing decision. I wanted a lifestyle in which I called the shots, regardless of how uncomfortable it felt at the time. In reality, living out your lifestyle the exact way you want should feel empowering, shouldn't it? Heck yes! We should be energized and invigorated by the choices we make in pursuit of our ideal lifestyle—otherwise, what is the point of it all? To commit to a career and increase our financial position only to not deviate until retiring at sixty? Or fifty-five if we're lucky? I chose right there to retire as an employee at twenty-five and, as Robert Kiyosaki says, get out of the "E" (Employee) quadrant and focus on the "B" (Business) quadrant.

I called my colleague back and said, "I'm going to Maui, and I don't think our current arrangement works anymore." I had a very close business and personal friendship with this person at that time, and I've always been a pain in his side because he loved organized chaos and always thrived in that environment. I, however, loved organized order, which helped me thrive and achieve top sales targets. We combined synergistically and kicked ass, although at times I'm sure my entrepreneurial blood and two-week vacation requests were a pain in his ass. Nonetheless, he knew it was my time to go for it, set up the lifestyle, and commit to making the business generate enough revenue to sustain me financially.

When I called Patrick back I told him I'd quit my job and was ready to go. Fast-forward twelve years later, and we still travel as best friends each year to Maui at least once, and some of our best ideas and experiences have come from stepping outside of our current home city circumstances to change up our environments for brainstorming and raising our frequency to bring in more abundance. I can say that had I stayed in one place and buried myself only in my business for the past twelve years without maintaining the importance of my lifestyle alongside the business growth, the company I built would not be at the level it's currently at, and my wellbeing and self-development wouldn't have advanced for me to evolve as a human being. That's what traveling does; it cultivates that curiosity and creativity to yearn for more in your life, to ask why the heck we have to force ourselves to feel like turtles in a shell geographically, like we don't deserve to get away somewhere for longer than the perceived norm. I encourage you to challenge your current lifestyle equilibrium and begin asking yourself: What is my ideal lifestyle? What does it really look like? Refer to your mental movie while doing it!

CHAPTER 19

Step on Can't

"Whether you think you can or can't, you're right."
—Henry Ford

Challenging the norm of letting negative thoughts dictate my energy level and behaviour, and controlling my attitude, was something I gave much thought to when I was eighteen years old. I knew this was going to be a huge limiting factor in my ability to achieve maximum potential, especially if I didn't get a grip on what the heck was going on in my brain on a day-to-day basis. If you really listen with curious receptivity to your own inner voice, you'll discover that we have dozens upon dozens of negative thoughts racing around in our minds every day! This had to stop for me, and I was going to observe this and identify exactly how to counteract what was happening, because this pessimistic skepticism and negativity was not going to be tolerated by my mind!

Isn't it interesting that our conscious minds start out prominently wired with negativity rather than positivity?

I'd think to myself quietly while thoughts of self-doubt and insecurity around the idea of failing as a human lingered, seeming to magnify my brainwaves as I simultaneously challenged the thoughts of my psyche. We have to change this wiring, or at least I had the compelling need to because of my upbringing, and I know I'm not alone in this. I began to train my mind to stop letting myself think that I can't do something. *Jevon, you can't afford this house. You can't build a business when you're older. Don't you know that you come from welfare and have drowned in poverty your entire life? Just be grateful if you don't starve each night, and if you have a warm bed to sleep on.* Believe me, I was grateful for this as I reflected on these thoughts. I realized that I was my own worst enemy, my biggest self-doubter out of all of them, as well as my biggest cheerleader. This all happened inside my own mind. I was fully in charge of steering the wheel and navigating how my attitude would be channeled internally, and how I'd behave externally.

It's a fascinating thing to know that we really do have the final say in what we do with our thoughts and whether we let the self-doubt seep in, drown our sense of self-worth, and cause the constant sensation of feeling emotionally drained. It's pretty easy to feel worthless if you allow it. A relationship goes sideways, a family loss, a relationship ends because you messed up—and believe me, we all mess up—and they moved on, and so on and so forth. You didn't get that job you wanted, or you got beaten out of a multiple offer situation on the property you've always wanted. It's easy to feel down and like you can't go on, so you might as well give up.

Manifest the Opposite, Positive Way of Thinking

There has to be another way, the ability to train your mind to think and say the opposite things. *I can afford this property, and no matter what, I'm going to create and attract so much success and abundance into my life that it's only a matter of time. In fact, my future success in all areas of my life is inevitable, damn it!* I said this to myself enthusiastically (I occasionally swear to pierce my subconscious). *I'm going to manifest the perfect relationship to eventually come into my life when the time is right.*

Validate and Then Dismiss the Negative Thoughts

I slowly learned that not only could I recognize the negative thoughts bouncing around randomly throughout my day, but I was completely in control of how long I should ponder that current thought. I was in control of validating the thought, and in turn building up psychological immunity to thoughts that actually are counterproductive to myself and those around me in terms of staying energetic, optimistic, and upbeat. I think the challenge for many people when listening to their negative self-talk is that they listen to it for way too long! It's like anything in life that we want—we have to work for it.

Training your mind to validate and then dismiss negative thoughts as quickly as possible is a mental exercise. It starts with writing some of them down throughout the day. Write down every one you remember in a journal for a few days on a daily basis, noticing how ridiculous the mind is unknowingly wired, based on our surroundings and interactions with people, to absorb and manifest negativity. You have to operate opposite of the norm, eventually muting out even social conversations with people you know when it seems that the subject of discussion is criticizing someone else who isn't present. Many people like to talk about what people lost; it seems to be a very deflating yet unusually enjoyable conversation. I'm baffled by the need for some to actually spend much of their own energy, which can be used on manifesting abundance and happiness, on the complete opposite. This is the silent killer of our dreams and aspirations, and many people aren't aware of this or they just honestly are unable to stop, as the "negative self-talk" is a learned human habit. If you're reading this book, there is a large part of you who wants to break out of their shell, or a part of you that already has and wants more. When we begin to learn about ourselves and how self-improvement impacts our well-being so positively, it becomes an incredibly addictive self-indulgence, because it's personality characteristic evolution, and that's what life is all about!

CHAPTER 21

Forgiveness and the Double-Edged Sword

"Forgiveness can be blissful."
—Anonymous

The relationship with my mother, or lack of one, created a lot of obstacles for me, primarily when it came to intimate relationships and fear of abandonment and commitment. I had been in relationships with a few unbelievably beautiful women, both inside and out, over the years, yet I could never give them all of me, as it meant risking being abandoned again, which would be far too painful. So I marched on, thinking that I'd eventually just find one that would work, without me really having to do that final emotional work required to be who I truly aspired to be as a partner. I didn't realize how unbelievably powerful the breakthrough was until I called my mother to tell her I'd forgiven her for everything. Wow. I was a changed man; understanding the need to forgive people in life is actually one of the biggest favours you can do for yourself as a human being. It can be unbelievably alleviating emotionally, and simultaneously so empowering.

Forgiveness can be beautiful; I think it's something that's required as one of the final steps before overcoming something substantial in your life. I felt for years like there was an invisible plateau I was comfortably operating on regarding my entrepreneurial and self-development spirit, athletic state, and emotional frequency. I knew I had a piece that could unlock more compassion and empathy in my life, and deep down I knew this could only be attainable by going back to a very painful point in my life, and it exists in many others lives as well. It's forgiving that person or persons who did you harm along the way. How dare they stunt our development, or almost handicap our development in some way, shape, or form from blossoming into our full identity at a normal human rate.

Watch Out for the Double-Edged Sword of Forgiveness

After forgiving my mother, I tried my hardest for a few months to have an over-the-phone relationship with her, as I thought it was really going somewhere. I thought I was getting through to her, helping her with her addiction. I tried adding pieces of inspiration I'd learned over the years, or telling her that all her children had forgiven her and were still in her life in one way or another, and the last to forgive was herself.

My mother at the time lived in a tiny trailer in Blackfalds. In my opinion, it's no place for any human to have to live. It was about one-quarter of the size of the trailers she used to live in before getting fully submerged in her addictions and really hitting rock bottom. She had recently committed to and completed a fair amount of rehab at the Ponoka Centennial Mental Health and Brain Injury Centre in Alberta, and I was trying to support her sobriety from alcohol and pain medication, along with other substances she may or may not have been on at the time. She'd get into crack cocaine years later, and her health and quality of life would really start to take even more of a nosedive, unfortunately.

A few months went by after building some emotional rapport with her, which was actually quite refreshing and meaningful to me. That quickly began to erode again once I started noticing her trying to mask her subtle incoherent behaviour while talking on the phone, slurring her words or repeating herself occasionally. It's very easy to tell when your loved one, especially a recovering addict, is "using" again. I can't explain the sickening and demoralizing feeling I felt once again listening to my mother relapsing. Although I now had this piece of forgiveness, which I am eternally grateful for, I realized right then and there that I don't need to own the idea of maintaining a relationship with someone you've chosen to forgive and still love. I decided to once again move into a healthy self-protection mode by creating a wellbeing barrier to protect myself from potentially maintaining a toxic relationship based on a subconscious family obligation.

We all know that a family obligation that's detrimental to our development is one of the hardest things to separate ourselves from, because love, loyalty, and blood are

About the Author

A serial entrepreneur, philanthropist, and real estate investor based in Calgary, Alberta, Canada, a competitive cyclist, triathlete, avid yoga student as well as instructor. On a perpetually relentless journey of self-development and spiritual awareness so that my true authenticity can be found. The goal in my life has always been to strive towards my most authentic self through healing from my upbringing, recognizing and learning how to manage our own triggers and behavioural patterns that can permanently hold us back from our ultimate fulfillment if we let them. I wrote the Vulnerable Alpha to provide a gateway for anyone who feels stuck in their own lives, whether it be emotionally or spiritually, to find internal inspiration to create a lifestyle of their choosing, regardless of one's past. I admire people who overcome adversity in their own lives and develop resilience to help inspire and lead others. My goal is to help inspire and motivate anyone who reads this book, knowing that you are seen, validated, honored and loved.